Exposed By DNA

A Path to Reveal

Family Secrets

I HOPE YOU ENJOY MY STORY!
KS Hopkins...

K.S. Hopkins

Dedication

For Karen, I wish you were here to see the end, my friend.

Acknowledgments

Thanks to my wife for all the loving support she has given me through all of this. I could not have done this without her. My friend Janet, you are like a little sister to me. Thank you for all your time and dedication to helping me. I am grateful to all my friends and those friends who shared their personal stories with me. My siblings, this will always be a journey and story we all took together. Alice, thank you for getting me started and making edits and suggestions along the way. My friend Liz, thanks for encouraging me to keep writing, and all the editing to help me finish.

Artwork by K.E. Hopkins
Foreword by Richard Hill

Table of Contents

Foreword by Richard Hill

"All families have secrets—some bigger than others." Those are the first words in my book, Finding Family: My Search for Roots and the Secrets in My DNA. However, they would also fit this story by K.S. Hopkins.

Genetic genealogy DNA tests helped me uncover the long-buried secrets behind my birth. Now, many years later—with vastly bigger databases—countless more family secrets are being uncovered daily.

Many people know their family mysteries up front, as in the case of adoptees searching for biological roots. Other mysteries present themselves unexpectedly to shake the most basic beliefs in our family history.

Exposed by DNA demonstrates once again that a combination of the right subjects, the right tests, and dogged persistence can uncover relationships that would otherwise remain buried by the sands of time.

Richard Hill

DNA-Testing-Adviser.com

Introduction

My journey begins when I find an innocent love letter my father wrote my mother in 1954. Who would have thought this little piece of history would change my entire family?

More people today want to know their ancestors' roots because of television shows and social media. Of course, many of us have heard stories from our families that made us even more curious about our families and our heritage.

With the use of many DNA sites, including Ancestry.com, 23andMe, GEDmatch.com, FTDNA, and My Heritage, I have been able to map my own DNA to discover family secrets. GEDmatch.com has been in the news for its role in identifying the "Golden State Killer" suspect. I have used this website to find answers with my own DNA.

My journey, described in this book, began as I turned fifty years old. More than half of my life has passed, but only now are my family's secrets coming to light. At first I was hesitant to write, but as more happened, I knew I had to tell my story. I wanted to show how we may learn family secrets, and what happens when we discover these revelations. The dynamics of each family will change depending on the type of revelations that occur.

My story begins with the dynamics of my family. I became interested in family genealogy after my father started learning his heritage. I was inquisitive about our history and wanted to know as much as I could about our ancestors. My father and I began studying our family's history together. I enjoyed spending time with him and discovering my roots and hearing his stories.

That is when an innocent love letter written in 1954 started a chain of events that laid the foundation for an exploration of the dates of paternity for my sister, Lucy. I never expected these secrets in my own family.

Before reading the love letter, I had already completed a DNA test with Ancestry.com to get more details on my own ethnicity. Who knew that after all my siblings completed their own DNA tests we would learn such shocking facts. Are there more half-siblings in our family? More secrets kept coming out when I least expected them. As shocking facts continued to surface, how would we handle the situation?

Science, in this case, has revealed what our parents never told us. Four siblings with different DNA?

My parents have kept secrets for more than fifty years. They both chose to keep quiet; now, I have learned that my mother is withholding more information—including secrets she never revealed to my father.

I am a happy person, blessed with many wonderful friends who have helped me stay focused. I am writing this book to help others gain the courage to explore their backgrounds, and then take what they have learned and grow because of this new knowledge.

How we handle the information we receive can make us stronger or break us. I choose to be strong. I view what I am learning as a continuing adventure. Keeping a positive perspective about my life and my relationships enables me to have the energy to meet new challenges. I have learned that we can't redo the past, but we may be able to learn from it.

Only now can I begin to peel back the layers of lies my family told me. However, we siblings still protect our parents and don't reveal to them what we already know. We do not want to hurt either parent.

I feel the need to stop the pattern of lies that has persisted all these years. Though my parents have always been poor communicators, this goes far beyond a lack of communication. The revelation of these lies has changed our lives forever. We still will have to see what will occur when more information gets exposed. We wonder whether changes will occur in how we relate to each family member. Unmasking the lies may lead us toward new directions in life.

To keep individuals' lives confidential, I have changed everyone's name. However, I have not changed the circumstances nor made up any stories. This book is all true except, as one of the crime shows used to say, "The names have been changed to protect the innocent."

Chapter 1: Growing Up and Genealogy

Everything seemed so easy when I was growing up. When I was asked to fill out forms and state who my parents were, I said: "Marilyn is my mother and David is my father." My siblings also answered the questions on the forms the same way. I never realized how everything that I had assumed would get so turned around after DNA analysis.

But, let's start from the beginning. In my immediate family, there are four siblings and our parents. My sisters are Lucy and Denise, and we have one brother, Greg. Lucy is the oldest sibling; I am the youngest. The order of our ages starting with the first child is Lucy, Denise, Greg, and me. There is almost a twelve-year difference in age between Lucy and me.

As a result of the age differences, I don't remember much of my childhood with Lucy. She was out of the house and married when I was six years old. She married her high school sweetheart, Rob, and they are still happily married today and have two children. I can remember Lucy and Rob together when I was young, but I can't remember living in the same house with her.

Denise is ten years older than I am, so I do remember more of her. At one time, when we were children, Denise and I shared a bedroom. She eventually moved down to the basement, where she had her bedroom and bathroom. I used to spy on her and her friends while they sat in her room smoking cigarettes. She had a little area with a sofa, almost like an apartment. I'm not sure why I remember spying on them. I guess even then I was interested in finding out things and not having secrets.

One summer day, Denise and one of her friends were sunbathing in our backyard. They were trying to get a nice suntan when a large crow flew overhead and pooped on Denise. She screamed and ran into the house and straight into the shower. As the mischievous youngest child, I laughed very hard at that situation. Several years later, Denise married Jim, and they have a daughter, Carol, and a son, David.

My brother, Greg, is about six years older than I am. He was around a lot more than either Denise or Lucy when we were growing up. He had his friends, and I had mine. Sometimes, we would fight, as siblings do. He would chase me around the house.

One day, Greg hid in my sister Lucy's car, a Buick Skylark. She started driving down the road when Greg jumped out from the backseat and scared her. Lucy became enraged with Greg. She still talks about that incident today—except today we all can laugh about it.

My parents were both working full time as I grew up. They would leave early in the morning and get home in the early evening. My mother worked for the military, and my father was a civil engineer. It was unusual during her career for my mother to have held the position she had without a college degree. My mother received a military driver's license and a forklift license. She would talk about how often the military police (MPs) stopped her when she was driving a military vehicle. I guess they had never seen a woman drive a military vehicle before. Eventually, they got used to her driving, and they left her alone.

When I was young, I spent a lot of time with my neighbor who babysat me. Several kids in this neighbor's family were my age. All of us kids became quite close, like brothers and sisters. Even the kids at school thought I was related to the neighbor's kids. I would walk down the hallway in school, and someone would ask me where my brother or sister was. I knew they were talking about the neighbor's kids, not my "blood-related siblings." My siblings often joked that I belonged to the neighbor's family.

Each morning when I was growing up, my father would make me breakfast before school, and he made sure I got on the school bus. My mother had to leave for work very early in the morning. After school, I would go to the neighbors' house until my parents came home from work.

During my childhood, we always had at least one dog in our house. My father had compassion for dogs and taught me the same kindheartedness. As an adult, I had a dog named Willy for eighteen years. He lost his eyesight at age five due to a common health problem in his breed. The vet removed both of his eyes.

Despite all his handicaps, Willy was amazing. He ran, swam, hiked, and did just about everything a dog with eyes could do. He learned commands so he could avoid running into objects. I used to put stickers on his face where his eyes should be. These stickers seemed so natural that they became a joke among my friends. I will always treasure the time Willy and I had together. I wish that dogs had more years on earth. They teach us so much about compassion and love. My dad still has a dog, and they go hiking every day.

Besides having a love of dogs and other animals, my father had a great love of the outdoors that he passed on to me. My father always let me try things and learn on my own. If I failed at something, he told me it was okay, and he made me feel better.

My mother was the one who bandaged me when I hurt myself and protected me as the youngest child. She taught me right from wrong and to be polite and respectful. She played cards and board games with me at night. My mother worked all day, but she made sure dinner was on the table every evening after she returned from work. She made sure all my siblings and I had positive relationships with our grandparents, aunts, uncles, and cousins.

Back in the 1990s, I started to help my father in his genealogy research and became interested in my family's origins.

3

Never in my life did I anticipate that my genealogy would be a puzzle. When I started researching our family history with my father, I was in my twenties. My father started the ball rolling, and I took some interest here and there. When we first began doing genealogy research, I was not completely on board. I much preferred going out and spending time with my friends. However, I always enjoyed hearing family stories, and the more I heard, the more hooked I became, and I wanted to learn about where our family came from and who they were. I wanted to solve the mystery of our ancestry and learn more about the people in these stories.

From what I can tell, many people do not get interested in genealogy until later in their life—maybe in their forties. Perhaps as a young person, I was only concerned about the future and did not consider that the past was important. I can now see how revelations about the past have changed the trajectory of my life.

Psychologists have shown our memory of the past strongly influences our ability to envision the future.[1] We tend to use memories of past experiences to predict what our life will be like in the future, which is why it helps to know what has happened to our family in the past—in other words, why genealogy is important. We want to know not only about the successes in our family but the failures and disasters as well. We can use our ability to envision the future to help us make plans. Our beliefs about what might happen in the future help us to plan for problems that may confront us.

Research on planning suggests that people who prepare for failure are the ones best equipped to handle problems when they come up. If you have never experienced failure or major problems, then when you are confronted with problems, you may not know

---

[1] Art Mattham, "Your View of the Future Is Shaped by the Past." *Psychology Today.* Aug 12, 2011 https://www.psychologytoday.com/blog/ulterior-motives/201108/your-view-the-future-is-shaped-the-past.

how to cope with them. And our past also has a great influence on what happens in our future. The education we get, the friends we make, and the careers we choose all exert a strong role in how our adulthood plays out.

Catastrophic events, such as the death of a family member, can make us realize that we have lost an opportunity to get questions about our family answered. I wish I had listened more to family stories when I was younger. As I grew up, I became more interested in how each of the children in my family of cousins was related to me.

My father learned that his great-grandfather's side of the family came from a small, quite charming town called Waterford, which is located in Virginia. We have visited this town many times while doing our genealogy research. My father would also show me where his parents and grandparents were raised. He pointed out houses they lived in and told me stories about them. We walked through many cemeteries; he told me tales and showed me where our relatives were buried. On these visits to cemeteries, we obtained information from tombstones, to learn dates of birth and death.

The family was Quaker. My father's great-grandfather was kicked out of the Quaker church because he would not marry a young lady who he had gotten pregnant. His family apparently tried to get his brother to marry her. My father's great-grandfather ended up leaving Virginia and headed to Maryland, where he married a different woman and raised a family. We never found out the details of what happened to the children he left behind. Some records show she had twins, a boy and a girl.

Doing genealogy research with my father gave me the opportunity, as an adult, to learn more about him and his childhood. We took many trips around town to different historical societies, libraries, and cemeteries. We looked through documents in big, old, heavy books; used microfiche machines; and examined anything we could find that had a familiar surname. We also would talk to anyone who might know the local history. Both of us will talk to just about anyone—we share this trait, which is different from my mother, who is more aloof.

I liked these trips because I got to spend time with my father and share his interest in what I thought was my family. Our objective was to try to build a story of how our family arose. It was like a jigsaw puzzle, but we didn't have all the pieces.

We always wondered: Why did our ancestors do what they did? Why did they come to this country? Did they know anyone when they came? Why did they settle where they did? Why did my father's family come to Virginia in the first place? What was there for them?

Some of the documents we researched provided clues. My father's side of the family was old, to begin with when he was young. He always told me, "They were so old, I mean old."

I was working full time when I first started doing genealogy with my father. I didn't have much time to get as involved as I wanted. However, I tried to help as much as I could and retain as much information as my father was telling me. I probably should have tape recorded some of his stories or insisted that he write them down.

He would relate stories of his childhood and family life. He was the only boy from a family of four children. He grew up in Laurel, Maryland. His mother, my granny, had lots of sisters. The sisters all hung around the house when my father was growing up. Several of them lived in the same house. All of his mother's siblings were very close.

When I was growing up, I also saw the closeness between my granny and her sisters, my great-aunts. I don't remember my great-uncles. I think many were dead, or they were divorced. However, I adored my granny and all my great-aunts. We had a lot of cousins growing up and spent much time with them.

The meeting place every weekend was at my granny's house. My father's father, my grandfather, died when I was about ten years old. He used to sit us grandchildren on his knee and tell us stories and sing to us. My father told me that when he was a youngster, his father would get angry and go into their attic and haul out boxes of old photos and documents. He would burn them in their yard. It seemed my grandfather had a temper and did not care about preserving history—the total opposite of my father and me. We both love history and want to preserve it. I don't remember too much of grandpop, but apparently, according to family, he could be very mean and might have been a little crazy.

There may have been a reason my father's dad burned the family photos and records beyond having a bad temper. Perhaps there were things that he wanted to hide. He may have had his secrets.

While doing genealogy research, we found that my father's grandfather was a member of the Maryland House of Delegates in the 1890s as a Republican. It makes me laugh to think he was a Republican because my father is very much a Democrat. However, the parties have evolved and changed over the years. Perhaps my great-grandfather was more of the true party of Lincoln than many of the Republicans of today. I wondered whether he was against slavery—most Republicans of the time were.

Growing up, I never talked politics with my father. Politics was a topic that never came up until I was much older. I always assumed my father was a Republican based on the old-school attitude he has today. Then, one day I was visiting at my parents' house, but my father wasn't home. I discovered, much to my surprise, that he was at a Democratic Party training session learning to be a poll volunteer for Bill Clinton's presidential campaign, which was the first of many surprising things I learned about my father, a man I thought I knew.

My mother never voted in her life. That has always upset me. How can she not vote? When my mother has said things over the years about politics and about who is in office, I always said to her, "You didn't vote." She does not explain why she has not voted; she shrugs her shoulders. I make the point to her—you have no right to complain unless you get involved and vote. I know that makes her angry. However, it does not make her angry enough to go out to vote.

My mother follows my father's lead in political views, even though she doesn't vote. She seems to believe what my father says. Some of my friends seem to follow the direction of their husbands. I tell them to think on their own. I urge them to do what they believe, and not be a follower, but to have their independent thoughts. That's what makes us all different.

Genealogy helps us discover similarities among members of the family and see patterns of behavior and health histories that might have a bearing on our life. While researching with my father, I discovered that his biggest unresolved genealogy question was finding out what happened to his great-grandfather. He seemed to have disappeared, with very few records of him. We could find no gravesite, no death certificate—but there were land records, and his wife's will mentions him as deceased.

We find it weird that he left very few records. My father thinks he was a crook and owed money, so he chose to leave little information. I think that my father was simply making up stories. Sheer invention is how a whole bunch of tales get told from family to family.

However, I am sure my father and I will keep searching for information on his great-grandfather, who remains a mystery to us. We have spent years trying to learn more about him and other members of the family. To do this, we read through old land records. In our county, land records are available online. Electronic information systems make it easy to research current and old property and get information on those who owned this property.

Land records will tell you everything, from where boundaries of the property are to names on old maps—names that might help in family searches.[2] They also can show the surnames of property owners and list old town names.

When my father and I were at the Maryland State Archives, a young man named John showed us how to access records online. We picked up a few other tricks on how to access records online and the ins and outs of researching as we went along. Now, accessing land records is easy for me. I find learning about and doing genealogy research is fun.

We do know that my father's great-grandfather operated a mill in the 1850s. We sometimes go hiking on the property where the mill once stood. It is not far from where my parents currently live, something we did not know until my father and I started our genealogy research. One day while hiking in the area of his old house, I found the foundation to the old mill. I dug up a lot of old bottles. Digging in the dirt made me feel like a kid again, even though at that time I was an adult. I then took out my metal detector and found the door to an old stove. I enjoyed the adventure of these excavations. If I had lived as a kid back then, this mill area with its hundreds of acres would have been a great place to play.

---

[2] An interesting tutorial on using land records for genealogical research is at http://www.lhaasdav.com/land/index.html.

Today, heavy briars make access to this area difficult. Next time I visit there, I will take a shortcut by crossing the river in front of the property. Otherwise, getting there requires about a mile hike through the woods. The Washington Suburban Sanitary Commission (WSSC), one of the largest water and wastewater utilities in the nation, owns part of his former property. In the 1950s, WSSC bought a lot of land near this ancestral property for building a dam. Some housing developments surround the old property.

Reading the land records from the mill property in the 1800s is quite interesting. The property originally belonged to my father's great-grandmother's family. The will of her parents divided the land among her siblings. After she married, the area maps show her husband, my father's great-grandfather, as the owner of the land. I can't imagine women today marrying and then having to put all their family property in their husband's name.

I am fascinated by how women's rights have changed over time. My research allows me to see how society trampled their rights during earlier eras. Women's rights are another manifestation of human rights.

I recall the visit of First Lady Hillary Rodham Clinton to the 1995 United Nations Fourth World Conference on Women, held in China. She said:

> By gathering in Beijing, we are focusing world attention on issues that matter most in the lives of women and their families: access to education, health care, jobs, and credit, the chance to enjoy basic legal and human rights and participate fully in the political life of their countries.

I enjoy seeing women finally coming into more important roles in history. I can't even imagine women not being able to vote back then. Perhaps this is why I get so angry at my mother for her not voting.

I suppose living in the 1800s was not easy. But maybe my ancestors would have hated life today with all the technology and with its different pace of life. Reflecting on my current life filled with cell phones, Internet access, and, of course, television, I realize that I do like our modern technology. I can't imagine being born in the 1800s, but I would not want to be a child in 2018. Society today seems too fast paced. If I were a child today, I think the pace of things would frighten me.

Growing up in the era when I did, life just seemed easy. I don't remember any bullying or violence. The times were not perfect by any means, but daily life didn't seem to have the types of battles we have now. People talked to and knew their neighbors, and just said hello.

I realized the other day when I was out walking, you can pass several people on the sidewalk, and people ignore each other. Very few people say a pleasant "hello" as you pass them. Younger teenagers rarely speak and say hello. I think, where are their manners? I always say "hello" to people; it's a respectful thing to do.

Modern technology has made us lazy. I can't understand why we need a car that backs up and parks for us. Park your own car. And, of course, our ancestors drove horses, not cars. It's interesting to think how the pace of life has changed and is continuing to change over the generations.

I also notice that when we go out to eat at a restaurant, cell phones absorb people's attention. You see families sitting together, and no one is talking; they all are on their phones. What happened to socializing? I want to yell: "Put your phones away."

Despite my complaints, I am glad for some of the comforts of our modern era. It would have been difficult to grow up without electricity in my home. I do hate when the power goes out. I like the convenience of having power and running hot and cold water. I could not imagine not having these conveniences. As a child, maybe I would not know better, but not as an adult.

I remember going to the outhouse bathroom at my mother's family's farm when we were kids, which was cool as a kid, but never now. And what about wandering to the outhouse in the bitter cold of winter? Besides, there could be snakes in there!

Despite snakes in the outhouse, I loved my childhood. When I grew up, we would play in the woods, build forts, and not come inside until it was dark. All the parents in the neighborhood had their own bell or whistle to indicate to their children when it was time for them to come home and eat dinner. Everyone knew their parents' distinctive call or yell.

A friend of mine posted a picture on Facebook today of a fort we had built as children. We would construct forts in the woods using branches from trees and sometimes camp out in them. Our forts reminded me of the houses on the television show *Gilligan's Island*, which was popular in the late 1960s. We were very creative as kids. Seeing this photo brought back lots of happy memories.

When I was a child, I would camp out for almost the whole summer in my parents' backyard. A group of us neighborhood kids either slept in a tent or under the stars. We would have campfires every night. Sometimes we would cook over the fire. We selected the firewood from the woods. We started these campfires with no assistance from our parents.

Sometimes, we would pour gasoline on the wood for an easy fire. It was scary doing that, and we didn't do it often after one time when we caught the grass on fire. Of course, our parents never knew anything about the gasoline. That was a secret that we now can reveal without hurting anyone.

This same group of kids would raid neighbors' gardens in the middle of the night. Then, we would eat fresh vegetables and fruit. It became a game to see who could get the best stuff. Life was easy, a few mischievous pranks, but nothing too bad. We knew our parents would get after us if we misbehaved too badly.

Another time when we were kids, my friend Janet and I got caught swimming in the neighbors' pool without permission. Our neighbors, who lived in a house behind ours, were not home. Their big house bordered the woods and had a long driveway. To get out of the intense heat, Janet and I decided to go swimming, well skinny dipping. No one could see us because the house sat way back on their property.

While we were in their pool, the neighbors returned home. We knew we should not have been there skinny dipping. So, both of us peeked over the edge of the pool and waited for their car to pull into the garage so we could jump out of the pool and run. When the car pulled into the garage, we jumped out of the pool, grabbed our clothes, and ran through the woods as fast as we could while trying to get dressed. We were laughing very hard, but we were scared that we would get caught.

However, we made it back to my house, and no one was home there. Janet quickly dried her hair with my hair dryer. Before she was finished doing this, her mother phoned and told her to come home. Under her mother's questioning, Janet denied getting in the pool, but her mother felt her hair, and it was still damp. She was grounded. I don't think my parents ever found out.

This "getting away with stuff" was typical of what happened to me. When I first went into law enforcement, my friends and cousins laughed at the thought of me in law enforcement. They always said I was a little troublemaker growing up, but I kept a straight face and acted as if I had done nothing wrong. However, I was always curious about everything going on around me, and I still want to know the "why" of everything.

Chapter 2: My Mother and Father: A Study in Contrasts

My mother couldn't care less about genealogy. Even as a kid, I don't remember going to see historic locations with her, only with my father. He would take us to museums and historic sites. He was interested in learning more about his background and his people.

My father would let us kids do almost anything. He let us swim in rivers and walk out on the iced-over river in the wintertime. I think that if my mother had seen us on an iced-over river, she would have killed him. My father didn't just take his kids, he would take any of the neighborhood kids who wanted to go.

Some of the neighborhood kids would get in trouble with their parents for swimming in the river. Their parents would get upset because their children came home in dirty, wet clothes. That didn't stop my father; he would still take everyone. He would tell all of us to have fun. I think he wanted us to enjoy life, as he did as a child. He did not seem concerned about what other parents thought.

He took us kids hiking, and these hikes helped me appreciate nature—especially the animals around us. Like my father, I see animals all the time that most people don't even notice. My father taught me to recognize different types of birds and to listen for their unique sounds. For example, while I'm driving, I notice everything out of the corner of my eye: owls, hawks, and deer. I point them out to whoever is with me in my car. My wife always comments: "How did you see that?"

My response: "Maybe I was an animal in a past life." I notice nature all the time, even down to a small rodent.

I still don't know how to distinguish poisonous mushrooms from others, or which berries are safe to eat. Oh, and I hate snakes. My father will pick up any snake that is safe, but I hate them.

By contrast, my mother would not walk out through nature. Instead, she would take my brother and me to Disney World in Florida. I never recall my sisters going, and my father never would go—not his idea of fun. He liked to be outside in nature, not at some amusement park.

My father was a social person. One thing that always made me laugh was that my father attends not only his high school reunion and party, but he will attend my mother's reunion and party without her, even though they are four years apart in age.

As a child, our whole family went to Point Lookout State Park in Maryland. This area in St. Mary's County is the most southern part of the state, at the confluence of the Chesapeake Bay and the Potomac River. It was the site of the largest and possibly most notorious Civil War prisoner of war camp. I have returned here several times. Though the area is beautiful, perhaps because of its history, it has always felt a bit spooky to me.

My father's sisters and their family accompanied our family. We stayed in an old run-down beach house on the water that belonged to one of my father's friends. While I was there, I went out on a speedboat and went swimming. I got stung by jellyfish across both legs while I was swimming.

The only other trip I recall my parents going on together was a trip to Michigan when I was a teenager. They went to see an older couple, friends of my father's, who lived on one of the lakes in Michigan.

As a child at the holidays, our entire family would be together on Christmas Eve. My parents would make beef fondue. It was fun to stick a hunk of meat on a metal stick and dip it in hot oil and watch it cook. Eating beef fondue was a family tradition for many years. Then, after we ate, we would play some board games as a family.

However, when this tradition stopped, we would get together with our entire family—grandmothers, aunts, uncles, and cousins for a holiday party at one of our houses. If we had the party at our house, my father would show home movies on the old 8 mm film with the old-time projector. We laughed at the movies each year though we had seen the movies over and over from years past.

Chapter 3: My Grandma and Granny: Two Quite Different People

My father's mother, who I called "granny," went with us on many vacations. My father, as I mentioned earlier, would not go— even with his mother. It was usually my mother and me. I would get to take a friend or my cousin, Samantha. Sometimes, my mom's mother, "grandma," would go with us. However, granny went most of the time. The two grandmothers never went at the same time.

I adored both of my grandmothers. My siblings and I spent a lot of time with our grandparents. I will always treasure those times. I usually would spend Saturday night at one of my grandparents' houses.

Grandma would always serve sherbet as a dessert. She would make us homemade chocolate chip cookies. She would mix the batter with her hands. She always had that one finger with batter on it, and she would stick it in our mouths. I still remember her fat knuckled fingers, which were crooked from arthritis. But, eating raw cookie dough was the best. It didn't kill me even though now children are advised not to eat it. We all lived to tell about how great it was.

Grandma always made us our favorite foods when we spent the night. I realized as an adult that is why I grew to like instant mashed potatoes. She made me mashed potatoes and sauerkraut all the time. Her version of salad was cucumbers and tomatoes cut up with gobs of mayonnaise mixed in a big bowl. We all loved it.

Grandma was a kind soul; she never said anything mean about anyone. She was very loving toward all her grandkids. She would get down on her hands and knees outside and play marbles with us on the sidewalk when we were kids. She loved to play board games, including Chinese checkers. She also was a religious woman, always reading her Bible.

She grew up in the country on a farm. She told us that she could not wait to get off that farm because she was bored and did not like that life. While looking through the family records, my mother gave me a letter my great-grandmother wrote to grandma. It explained that she had heard that grandma was married and she wished her well. Did they not communicate? Is there a family pattern starting this far back? It is weird to think that both my grandparents ended up in the same town, where my mother and father went to high school, which was where they met. After high school, my father entered the military, and my mother went to work for the military as a civilian employee.

My grandma and my grandpop divorced. My sister Lucy told me grandpop went out of the state to Florida and filed for a divorce. Lucy thought he was a jerk. I don't recall a lot about him. I do remember that he remarried and we visited him and his new wife in New Jersey. It was strange that grandma went with us to visit her ex-husband. I guess they stayed friends.

My mother told me that while she was growing up, her father was an alcoholic. I don't know if that factored in her parents' divorce. I never recall my mother drinking. However, she told me that she was proud that: "Never in my life did I ever try smoking a cigarette."

My father's mother, granny, loved to gamble, play bingo, go to horse races, and play cards. She cussed and made us laugh. After going to church on Sunday mornings, the entire family went to granny's house, where she prepared a big breakfast for all of us. Aunts, uncles, and cousins were there. Granny never went to church with us, nor did my father. I never really thought to ask why as a kid. I still don't know the answer to that one.

Granny traveled a lot with my mother alone. They went to London, and another time, they drove across the United States. My mother and my granny seemed to have a better relationship with each other than my parents had with each other. Did they share any secrets?

Interestingly, I never remember my father visiting his mother. We were at granny's all the time, but he was never there.

Granny stayed up very late at night. If you drove by her house and the blinds were down at 11:00 in the morning, you knew she was still sleeping and not to disturb her. The front door to the house was always unlocked. Sometimes I would go into the house and sit waiting for her to wake up so that I could visit.

Though I loved both of them, my two grandmothers came from very different worlds. I have one picture of both of my grandmothers together. I will always treasure this picture. I am not sure what grandma thought of granny or vice versa. I know granny tried not to curse around grandma. They seemed to get along at family cookouts.

Chapter 4: A Murder

My uncle, my mother's brother, has documented that side of the genealogy tree. I still want to do my own research and find answers to some unsolved mysteries. On my mom's side of the family, I learned that someone murdered my great-grandmother in 1931 in Hardy County in West Virginia. I believe it is still a cold case with no suspects. I researched this and found much information about the murder. I even have a copy of the police report. It is quite a story. Apparently, someone hit my great-grandmother over the head with a blunt instrument—a violent act.

My great-grandmother was born around 1871, and the crime happened in 1931. Her murder occurred when she was in her early sixties. It's particularly weird to think the victim was my great-grandmother, and we do not know who did it or why it occurred. I only wish someone would find some new leads and reopen the case file.

The house where the murder happened is still there and used as a hunting lodge. My uncle visited and took pictures a few years back. To me, "lodge" sounds like something nice, but this place is an old house that looks decrepit. It should be called a "hunting shack."

Based on the pictures, I think it is probably haunted (if you believe in that kind of stuff, as I do). I would think with such a violent crime; my great-grandmother's spirit would be stuck there. I base that on my own beliefs. I think if I were a spirit, I would want to stay, probably just to scare people. Boo!

Chapter 5: Ancestry

I joined Ancestry.com in 2016 because I wanted to learn more about my ethnicity. I kept seeing their commercials on television, and I decided I wanted to submit my DNA and get back some answers about who I was and learn more about who my relatives were.

My wife also wanted to get her DNA tested to see her ethnicity. I purchased a membership with Ancestry.com to help me with my genealogy and family search. It seemed that through their resources, I could gather more facts. And, I thought, why not create a family tree to make things easier for myself?

My friend Karen allowed me to play a little on her Ancestry.com account before I joined, so I could see what the site had to offer. Members can search surnames, see census records for different countries, and view military records. Members can view other families' family trees to help guide them. There is an incredible amount of information here. An increasing number of records are available each day.

When the DNA results came back for my wife and me, they were not too much of a shock to me, since I knew many of my ancestors came from Germany and France. However, there were a few surprises. The results listed some other locations where some of my ancestors had lived, such as Italy, Greece, and Great Britain. Maybe my Italian roots help explain why I like red wine?

Ancestry.com has a clear ethnicity chart that allows you to see with whom your DNA matches. Matching DNA means that someone is related. The site matched me with a long list of cousins, from third cousins to many more distant cousins.

Now, having my own account with Ancestry.com, I was able to do more research. If I want to, I can go to each DNA match and see if the person provided a family tree. Seeing these trees could help us discover other ancestors we might not have known. It also can help us verify the information we already have. They can be used as a guide since they provide a great deal of information. We can make many discoveries by using the tools they provide.

I'm thankful that my wife and I are not related, based on our DNA results. It's not that I thought we could be related, since we grew up in different towns and knew none of the same people.

Chapter 6: My Father Gives Me His Genealogy Research and a Love Letter

Over a period of several months, when I visited my parents, my father had been giving me most of his genealogy research to take to my house. He was getting older and wanted someone to keep track of it. Since I was interested, I received his records and albums. He had put together all of the family albums and the documents that related to our research. Now, having the information at my house made researching easier for me.

He wanted me to have this stuff so I could continue to research if something happened to him or my mother. I was the only one of his four children who had an interest in genealogy. I told him that I would make sure that one of my nieces or nephews would end up with all the family history and documents so they could pass records down to their kids.

After bringing home several of his books, I had to get a new bookshelf that was big enough for all of his items. I treasured these items. I was not like his father, who burned all the records. I was proud of the relatives who I discovered, and I wanted to know more about them.

While he was giving me all this stuff, my wife and I were in the process of moving into a new house. We now had all these books and history he had given me. Usually, people want to get rid of stuff when they move, not add more. We always seem to be different.

While looking through the documents my father gave me, I found a love letter my father had written to my mother after the Korean War, when he was in the Army. My parents were not married at the time and would soon marry after my father returned home. He had written in his letter that it had been a long time since seeing my mother and he could not wait to come home to be with her.

I didn't think much of the letter and its value, but after reading it again and noticing the date, I was quite surprised. I was not surprised that my father had the letter; he keeps everything he can that has sentimental value. He must have taken the letter from my mother at some point and placed it in the genealogy book. The letter surprised me by the date it showed.

My father came home in January; my parents got married in March, but how did my sister Lucy come to be born in June of that same year?

Something was not right. My father was not around for my mother to get pregnant when she must have conceived. He was in another state on the other side of the country. He was a civil engineer for the U.S. Army and was stationed in Alaska at that time.

Maybe he came home on a Thanksgiving break, and my mother got pregnant. However, reading the letter over and over, it appeared he had not been home in a long time.

At this point, I did have questions for my parents, but I would never get the opportunity to ask—not because they died. No, they are both still alive.

My niece Carol, Denise's daughter, was with me looking at documents when we found the letter. Carol said something to her mother about the letter and its date, and Denise decided to say something to our father about Lucy's paternity. I don't know what their conversation was all about or how it started, but I do know Denise told our father to tell Lucy the truth and tell Lucy who her father was. I think Denise wanted to get the truth herself, to get some answers. It did get things started.

As I mentioned previously, in our family, there are four siblings: Lucy, Denise, Greg, and me. Over the years, we all had noticed that Lucy had dark hair and brown eyes. The rest of us have brown/blonde hair and blue eyes, as do our parents. We siblings had always joked about Lucy not being from our family. Now, this love letter popped up, and we raised questions and wanted to know who Lucy's biological father was.

When my cell phone rang, I had just gotten into my car after leaving an appointment. I did not expect the phone call I got from my father. I always think something is wrong when he calls on my cell phone. He doesn't call that phone very often, but as your parents get older, when they call, you answer. We had a conversation I will never forget.

My father confessed to me that Lucy was not his biological child. He raised her and loved her as his own. Apparently, my mother was pregnant when he returned from the military. They married within a few months of his return, and Lucy was born a few months later.

He explained that he did not want anyone putting labels on Lucy, and he loved my mother, so he raised Lucy as his own child. He told me that no one else in the family knew, only my mother. And, then I asked: "Who was Lucy's biological father?" He claimed that he did not know who Lucy's father was; my mother would never tell him. A sibling joke about Lucy not being our father's child was now a reality. Who would have ever thought this was coming out now—so late in Lucy's life? Lucy was sixty-one years old, and she would soon be finding out this truth.

Learning about her heritage was a shock. Finally, we were all going to learn the truth. I couldn't believe my father was first telling me this information. It almost felt like a dream. I urged him to tell Lucy.

My friend Karen, who was in the car with me, heard everything. Karen and I have chatted about family for years. We have been friends for more than thirty years. She comes from a very large Catholic family where drama is always happening. With ten kids, there is always commotion. She also is the youngest in her family. My family is less than half the size of hers, but we still seem to have our own drama.

Karen and I proceeded to go out for lunch. She gave me her advice, which always made me feel better. She thought my father's action in raising Lucy was honorable, and he was still her father. Karen always makes a situation okay. I'm not quite sure how she does it. Perhaps she learned something about human relations and being positive as the last child of ten in a family.

Karen had a wonderful outlook on life. She was diagnosed with breast cancer years ago and given only a few months to live. It had been more than two years now, and she was still living her life. The doctors got her life expectancy all wrong. She is the strongest person I have ever known. Her illness made her stronger. Realizing the battle that she was fighting makes our troubles seem minor. Her cancer had now spread to her lymphatic system and her lungs, but she was still fighting. What would I do without her? I couldn't imagine the world without her in it.

As I mentioned, our parents are not the best communicators. I guess it is a generation thing. When we were children and even now that we are adults, our parents choose not to communicate about problems. Instead, they keep quiet about problems. They ignore things and act as if the problems or uncomfortable events did not exist. They have always done this. So, it was quite a surprise for my father to tell me about Lucy's paternity.

He spoke as if he were talking to a friend and giving information, which was not a conversation I believed he would ever have with me. I am still shocked by this call.

Lucy did not know the truth about her biological origins. She also did not know that our father had told me the truth about her paternity—that she was not our father's biological daughter. Now, that the truth was out to me, my question was—what do I do with this information? Do I call her?

I have learned that, often, time has a strange way of solving problems—sometimes in unexpected ways. I told my wife what happened and asked her advice. She agreed that it was our father's story to tell Lucy. My wife and I said nothing to anyone about this. It was a family secret. I hate family secrets now more than ever.

My father wrote Lucy a letter to explain the situation. Why our mother was still quiet about all of this, I will never understand. She has not said a word and won't discuss it, according to our father. My father first tried to talk about this in person with Lucy. Lucy, I believe, did not want to have any conversation with him. After all, she was sixty-one years old and only now finding out this truth. I would be upset too. So, my father ended up writing Lucy a letter and explaining himself.

After Lucy read his letter, and now that the secret was out, Lucy called me and told me what she had just learned. I said that I knew about her not being our father's biological child.
I told her that our father had called me and talked with me, and that I had said I thought he should be the one to tell her. News of her paternity was his story to tell, not mine. I am glad he stepped up to the plate and explained things to her.

I still believe it was admirable for my father to raise Lucy as his own daughter. He loved our mother and married her, knowing that she was pregnant with someone else's child. Though, I wish that my parents would have told all of us children the truth. It was not fair to Lucy to find this out so late in life.

I still think my not telling Lucy first was the right thing to do. Now, if he would not have written her a letter or told her in person, then I would have had to tell her that secret. I did not want to be in that situation.

Realizing that Lucy now knew the truth was a relief. It seems that knowing has made her feel better. A lifetime of wondering about your background, but not knowing, can weigh on a person. The uncertainty of something like this is a big deal. Now, the secret was out. Then, the next question was—what do you do about it?

Chapter 7: What Do We Do Now?

Over the years, as I have mentioned, we had joked about Lucy not looking like any of us. We also had joked that her father was this man James, who our mother knew when we were kids. Lucy and I both remember James being around. I remembered him from when I was in early elementary school, and Lucy remembered him from when she was in high school.

There is that twelve-year difference in ages between Lucy and me, so this man James was around a long time. Could he be her biological father?

When James passed away, my mother sent me his obituary in an email and asked if I remembered him. She didn't send it to Lucy—just to me. I always felt her sending me the obituary was a bit odd. At the time, I thought nothing of it. She had not spoken about James in years.

As a joke, I emailed the obituary to Lucy and said something smart. I told Lucy that it looked like her father had passed away. I don't think she found it amusing. I only did it as a joke. We had joked about him being her father all these years. No one ever knew this could be a reality.

Now, the question remained, was he her biological father? The question of paternity was no joke. Lucy and I talked about this and felt convinced that James could be her father.

I even got on Ancestry.com and searched for a family tree for James. You can go to Ancestry.com's search tools and find other people searching the same surnames. You usually will have to look through lots of names and try to connect the dots. You have to see who lives where and figure out if you are even looking at the right surname link for the family you are searching. It helped that I knew the area where James had lived.

I told Lucy that if it were me, I would send my DNA to Ancestry.com and try to find my biological father. I also would ask our mother, "Who is my biological father?" Lucy did not feel comfortable talking to our mother about any of this. Our father already said our mother would not speak of it. I told Lucy, it would be harder to find the answers on Ancestry.com without her help.

I informed Lucy that since I was on Ancestry.com, I would help her in her search. Maybe we could find her biological father or that side of the family on their site. If Lucy would take a DNA test through Ancestry.com, I could try to match her with the DNA matches that come up on this site under her DNA test results.

She agreed and decided to get her DNA tested. Then, the waiting game for the results began. What I expected to happen was that Lucy would have DNA that matched with other people on Ancestry.com. Of course, I hoped that the DNA matches would show close relationship matches. And, a close match meant a close family tie, such as a parent or a sibling. Lucy could get a match with a first or second cousin, and so forth. Then, I would try to contact the closest matches and find the answer. I posted Lucy's information on my Ancestry.com account. When the results arrived, Lucy had several DNA matches.

The closest DNA match was, of course, me. I knew we were related, but now, I realized I was only her half-sibling, which was a joke between the two of us in light of the situation. I am listed as "Close Family," a sibling, as I should be. We do have the same mother for sure.

Ancestry.com shows your DNA matches in sections. The section where my DNA matched Lucy's was "Close Family." Then, Ancestry.com has sections for first cousin, second cousin, third cousin, and so on.

From all the DNA matches, I had to pull out the matches we both had on our mother's side. To accomplish this, I clicked on a link, which showed shared matches. I then eliminated matches that we both shared on our mother's side.

By doing this, I knew the new matches I was looking at were on Lucy's biological father's side and did not have anything to do with our mother's side of the family. The closest match for her from her biological father's side was DNA from a female third cousin. This third cousin had a family tree I could search, which made this job easier.

After looking at the matches from this cousin's family tree, I tried to figure out who Lucy's biological father could be. Given the third-cousin relationship, I realized that Lucy must share a great-grandparent with this cousin with whom she shared DNA. Ancestry.com showed a predicted relationship next to her match to explain what the relationship connection could mean.

Lucy and this cousin shared a great-grandparent. After about a week of research, I narrowed down who her father could be to a few potential family members. I did this winnowing down by looking at the family tree for the third cousin with whom Lucy matched on Ancestry.com. I took those great-grandparents' names, then looked at their kids to figure who her biological father could be, based on his age. After I had located some potential matches, the next step was to contact a complete stranger and ask for help.

I sent this unknown third cousin, Margaret, an email with the hope that she would respond. Her response came quickly. Now, I had some help in trying to figure out who Lucy's biological father was. After only one day, I received another response from Margaret. She was able to narrow the search down to two possible cousins who could be Lucy's biological father. She said she would help and get back to me.

Margaret made some phone calls and found Lucy's father. Lucy's biological father was Robert, one of Margaret's cousins. She contacted Robert, and he told Margaret our mother's name without her even saying it. He admitted he knew that our mother had a child, but he did not know Lucy was his child.

Margaret helped put Lucy and Robert in touch after all these years of not knowing each other. I know it was strange for Lucy to talk to her biological father for the first time.

We will always be grateful for all of Margaret's help in finding Robert. We were surprised how quickly we were able to get this information. The sad part is that none of us is getting any younger, and this discovery occurred so late in life. A new part of Lucy's family, Robert was very open and could not wait to meet his daughter, Lucy, for the first time.

Lucy and her husband, Rob, now needed to tell their children all that had been going on. It would be strange, I was sure, for my nieces and nephews to hear that they have another grandfather who was Lucy's biological father.

Lucy and Rob's kids took the news well. They were not surprised; I think because we all had joked over the years about how Lucy wasn't really a part of the family. Kids pick up little bits of information and hear rumors. They agreed to keep this news within their family and not to mention a word to their grandparents. They still would have the same relationship they had with all their grandparents.

Lucy and Robert now email back and forth. We also discovered that Lucy's new uncle (Robert's brother) currently lives not far from her home. What a small world.

Her biological father, Robert, lives in another state. He came to visit Lucy about a month after emailing and talking with Lucy on the phone. It was a great reunion. Robert got to meet Lucy, her husband, Rob, and their kids.

Looking at pictures of Robert, it was hard to believe how much he and Lucy resembled each other. Their looks told the story. Lucy has Greek and Armenian in her ethnicity. Now, we know why she tans so well in the summer at the pool. They both have a certain sense of humor that is much the same. Both Lucy and her biological father are very happy to have a new relationship. Everything is working out.

I am so happy for Lucy. She has a smile on her face that wasn't there before.

The sad thing is, Robert told Lucy that our mother told him that Lucy was not his child when Lucy was born. It is hard to think our mother did this. She kept Lucy's paternity from Robert all these years. She still keeps this a secret now. Little does she know, Lucy and I know the truth.

One of Lucy's half-brothers had already passed away before she got a chance to meet him. I blame her not meeting him on family secrets. She does have another half-brother she is getting to know.

Our two siblings, Denise and Greg, do not know anything about Robert. Lucy wanted to meet Robert before she told anyone else. They will know in time. Keeping this secret now from our other two siblings is very hard to do.

I believe the universe made Lucy and Robert connect, and this secret came out for the good. Things in life tend to happen when you least expect them, which was a good thing to have happened for Lucy.

So, now we know James, who was around us as kids, is not Lucy's father. We were both surprised.

Chapter 8: The Twist and the Turn

After everything that had just happened with Lucy, she suggested we have our father do a DNA test. This way we could double check and make sure he was my father. Of course, I thought this was highly unnecessary. After all, I looked like the other members of my family and had no reason to suspect otherwise.

However, my DNA was already in the Ancestry.com database. We discussed having our other two siblings get their DNA tested, just to verify all paternity, which seemed like a good idea, I thought. This way, there were no questions, since our parents seemed to keep secrets.

Nobody in our family questioned anyone else's paternity just Lucy's. Lucy told me she and Rob, her husband, had discussed the idea that my father may not be my biological father. They thought that I should have my DNA compared to his just to double check. It seemed a little farfetched to think I was not his child. However, once Lucy put this thought and question in my mind, I decided to forge ahead and find out.

The more I thought about it, the more interested I became. My father and I are different in many ways, but we also have many of the same passions. How much of our passions and interests were based on genetics as opposed to our environment? We both love genealogy, history, and nature, and we are passionate about our love for dogs. At this point, I was sure he was my father.

Now that Lucy had me interested in thinking about the DNA results, could I get my father to do his DNA test without telling him what I wanted it for? Lucy had confirmed her biological father; now, I felt as if I needed to be sure he's my father. Lucy has put this thought in my head. I don't want to upset him with all of this. I can't just ask him to do the test for this reason. I do not want to hurt him.

I had an idea, yes, a little sneaky, but I thought it should work. I would have my father do the DNA test as an early birthday present. He loves genealogy, so I could get him an ethnicity chart. I would get his DNA, and get the results of his DNA from which I could make a large ethnicity chart, and put it on laminated paper. Ancestry.com provides you with a great map and chart of the countries of your ancestors. I decided to make it big so he could view it with ease. I thought he would be happy to get this so he could see where his family came from, and we would have the DNA to determine my paternity. As I mentioned, my DNA was already in the Ancestry.com database, along with Lucy's. We needed to see his DNA results to compare it with mine. If he were my father, as I suspected, this would show up in the Close Family category, and it would say he is my father.

My next step was to order the kit and wait for its arrival. The plan was going well. About a week later, the kit arrived by mail. I called my father and told him I had gotten him an early birthday present, and he needed to come to my house. He came fairly quickly, and I showed him his early birthday present, the DNA kit. He was happy to get it and looked forward to getting his results. He wanted to see his ethnicity.

The mail carrier happened to be there right after he completed spitting in the tube for the DNA kit. We boxed up his DNA sample and handed the package to the mail carrier. We had to wait about eight weeks to get his results. Waiting was the hardest part—especially for me. During this period, I spent time thinking—was he really my father? Thanks, Lucy and Rob!

Shortly after my father left, I called Lucy and told her that our father had already completed the DNA test. It was off in the mail. I still say he was Lucy's father; he did raise her, even though Robert was her biological father.

Our parents know nothing about Lucy and Robert meeting. Lucy wanted to keep that private. I am not sure why, but that was her choice. Lucy and I had different relationships with our father. She remembers bad times growing up, and I remember good times. There is that age difference between us. Maybe I am the youngest, and our parents got it right with me.

When I was a child, my father made me breakfast and got me ready to go to school. On most school mornings, we would eat our breakfast and watch the *Three Stooges* on television. We would laugh together. He also would take me hiking and camping. We had a good relationship growing up. We both loved the outdoors and did a lot of things together. Lucy and our father did not have this type of relationship.

I recalled one time, my friend Janet and I wanted to go camping, and my father promised he would take us after school on a Friday. We were both very excited. It was raining so hard that day, and it was supposed to rain all night. My father asked me if I still wanted to go. I was a kid and, of course, I said "yes."

When I was an adult, I realized that he probably did not want to go camping that evening because it was pouring rain and miserable outside. No one would want to be in the woods. Nevertheless, he still took us; he did it out of love. I'm sure.

I wish Lucy had more good memories of growing up with our father. It is sad to think she didn't. I can only tell her how I felt. I am not saying my father is perfect, by any means. He has made me angry on several occasions, but, he still is our father, and I am grateful for him being an important part of my life.

Chapter 9: The Results

I was watching television on Sunday morning when my phone beeped to let me know I had an email. The email reported that the results of my father's DNA test were now available. I immediately went to my office and checked the computer. There they were—my father's results.

My DNA page lists Lucy and me as half-siblings. We share the same mother. But where is my father in my group? He should be there. The results should say he is my father. This fact was not there! My sister Lucy and her husband, Rob, were right. He's not my biological father, either.

I couldn't believe what I was seeing. My first thought was—this can't be. I was shocked. I looked at the results again. They listed my father's first cousin under his DNA results. He was a match to her, but not me. I should match both of them, but I did not.

At that moment, I felt both shocked and lost. I told my wife the results. She was shocked. She told me she was sorry. I couldn't believe this was happening—the man who raised me was not my biological father. What had my mother done?

Since we had scheduled a lunch date with some friends, I did not have time to look at the computer any longer. I could only think to myself, what should I say? It felt as my world was crashing in on me. My stomach was in knots. How should I act?

All I could think of was all the funny jokes Lucy and I had told each other the last few weeks while waiting for the DNA results. We were joking and saying the names of those who could be my "daddy." Our joking around was all in fun. Now, the truth was out. My father was not my biological father. What would Lucy say to me now?

I needed to act happy at lunch. However, all I wanted to do was sit and process this. Then, the doorbell rang. No processing time for me.

We went to brunch at a local pub we like. We were all chatting, but I felt quite emotional about the DNA results. I didn't want to act differently; I didn't want to say anything, but, this information was all I could think about at the moment.

The friends we were with at brunch were friends of my wife—a girl she grew up with and her mother. Her mother was about my parents' age. She was a very sweet lady, and while she and I were talking, my story came out.

I said aloud: "My father is not my biological father, I just found out ten minutes before you came into our house." We talked about this for some time. I am sure she saw the shock on my face. All I thought was, I just told this woman my business. Was she going to think I was crazy? She looked a bit shocked when I told her this information.

I think she was trying to keep my mind occupied and make me feel better. We talked about times when she was young and how things were different then for women. She talked a lot, but I don't remember much of the conversation. I think I was hearing but not retaining any information. She said something about how women kept quiet and were not as outspoken as they were today. She asked questions about my family, and I tried to answer the best I could in my dazed state.

I was feeling as if I were hearing everyone, but the world did not make sense. It was as if I had just gotten off a carnival tilt-a-wheel and was unable to balance. I had that dazed feeling during the rest of lunch. However, I tried my best not to show it. I kept telling myself, laugh, keep smiling. Any emotion I felt about my discovery would need to wait.

When my wife and I returned home, we sat down to talk about my discovery. She told me to call Lucy and give her the news. I called Lucy and told her about the DNA results. I think Lucy was surprised at hearing the words come out of my mouth, but she was not surprised by the results.

Lucy and Rob had talked about this before. Apparently, they thought this would be the result. They didn't know the truth; they just had a gut feeling. But now, I am surprised at the truth.

Lucy wanted to know what I was going to do. I told her that I was going to confront our mother with the DNA results, and what this has revealed. To allow myself some time to process this new information, I decided that I would wait until the next day to talk with my mother.

I think Lucy was a bit shocked that I would confront our mother. I explained to Lucy; I needed to know the answers now. I was not going to wait until it was too late to question our mother.

Lucy brought up the name of James again. Now, this made me think, could James, my mother's friend, be my biological father? He was not Lucy's father as we first thought. He was around as we were growing up. Was he my biological father? My mother did send me his obituary years ago; this had me thinking.

I felt very confused. I kept thinking and telling myself—the man I called my father was still my father; he raised me. He was and is a good father.

I am not sure why, but I am one of those people who need to know the answers. I have always needed to know the "what," "who," "when," "how," and "why." It was in my blood; it was part of my career.

My prior careers were in law enforcement and investigation. I still feel the need for answers to questions. I always seemed to dig into backgrounds of people. It is a habit I can't break. I guess I have always been this way. I have always been looking for that clue and the reason why. As a kid I was the same, I wanted to know the why of everything. I needed all the details.

I had many unanswered questions in my head. Should I be mad at my mother? Did my father know anything? Had they both been keeping this secret from me? Lucy's paternity had been a secret all these years. Were our parents keeping this from me, from all of us? Were there other secrets in our family? What do I do now?

I told my wife that I needed to talk with my mother tomorrow at their house. I needed to get my thoughts together. How would I approach her? What would I say to her? How would I lead up to the conversation? Do I just directly come out and ask? I would have to confront my mother without my father knowing any of this. I didn't know at this point who knew what. As I said before, my parents don't communicate well. It is hard for us to communicate with them. They make us feel uncomfortable.

I did not sleep well that night. Thoughts kept spinning in my head. Now, I knew how Lucy had felt all these years, feeling different and not knowing the truth. She hasn't slept well in years. I wonder whether her new knowledge allowed her to sleep better. Was it my time not to sleep well? Lucy has had a lifetime of uncertainty about her paternity; mine was only one day of knowing he was not my biological father.

The next morning, I drove to my parents' house. My brother, Greg, lives with my parents; I had to make sure he and my father could not hear the conversation I was about to have with my mother. My father was not home, so that was easy. Now, I had to get my mother alone, away from Greg, who was in the living room watching television. My mother told me she wanted to show me something in her bedroom, which was perfect. I could confront her now.

My mother has her share of health issues, which could make this a difficult conversation. I needed to tread lightly with her. However, as soon as we were in her room, everything spilled out of my mouth like a bomb that had exploded. I didn't realize how upset I was until I started talking about it with my mother. I flat out asked her, "Who is my father?" She gave me a blank stare. I told her, "I got my dad's DNA results back, and they didn't match me."

To my surprise, she said that she was afraid this would come out after we started doing DNA tests. I was so shocked she was saying this and asked again, "Who is my father?"

The conversation was not what I expected. My mother told me she did not know who my father was. She provided very few details, and I wondered if even these were correct. She made me feel even worse. She was very vague in her answers. I didn't know what to believe. I was in shock all over again.

I explained to her that I needed to know the answers for health reasons. Were there any hereditary diseases I need to be aware of? All these crazy thoughts were churning through my head.

Was she not telling me because something awful happened to her and she didn't want me to know? What was happening here?

I told her that I knew the truth of who Lucy's biological father was. I told her that his name was Robert and that Lucy now knew the truth. My mother stared at me, and I continued talking. She did not agree or disagree with me telling her Lucy's father was Robert. I told her that I figured it all out thanks to the DNA test from Ancestry.com. My mother looked shocked but said nothing.

I was in shock myself. I realized that I had just told my mother that I knew who Lucy's father was. However, I had told Lucy that I would not tell our mother anything about Robert. My emotions had spilled out more in anger than anything else. We say a lot of things we shouldn't say when we're angry. I remembered the sensible idea of not calling my ex-girlfriends when I had been drinking. I knew that in those cases, I might say things I shouldn't.

I thought Lucy was going to be angry at me for telling our mother about Robert. I always knew our sister Denise had no filters on her mouth, but me—I had let it all out.

My mother never did give me a name or any good information that would help me know who my biological father could be. I asked my mother—did my father know any of this? She told me that he didn't know and that he has been a good father to me. Was she saying he was a good father to me so I should keep her secret?

I told her I would not say a word to him about any of this. I did not want to break his heart.

I walked out of my parents' house in a state of shock, filled with more unanswered questions. As I walked away from the house to my car, my father pulled into the driveway.

I waved at him, got in my car, and pulled away. He had a quizzical look on his face, and he probably wondered why I did not talk to him. I felt so mixed up. I knew he was still my father no matter what the DNA test revealed. He raised me—not some stranger.

At this point, I couldn't face him or talk to him. I had a secret that I had to keep from him, and I didn't want to break his heart. How could I tell him he was not my biological father? I thought it would crush him, and I was afraid he would be mean to my mother if he knew the truth.

By not telling my father, I was trying to protect my mother. This whole situation was very confusing. I did not want to be upset at my mother due to her precarious health state. I didn't know how to feel. Never in a million years did I think that I would be feeling so empty inside.

I am not the type of person to get in a "funk." I have always tried to stay positive in any life situation, but this was a very unusual situation, and I felt blank. Nevertheless, I promised myself to keep going and try not to let this take over my emotions and ruin my life.

I was puzzled by my mother's ability to lie all these years. Why would she do that? It makes me question her love for her kids. Do we matter to her? Did we ever? Many thoughts raced through my head—especially about my mother with all these lies. I wondered whether keeping these secrets was worth it for my mother.

If she were unhappy in marriage, why didn't she get out? If I had been unhappy, I would have changed my life. And, in other situations, I have done this. I was in a long-term relationship and was not completely happy as I thought I should be. I made a huge change, sold our home, and moved.

I bought a house all by myself and started my life over, which was probably one of the hardest things I had ever done. It took a lot of courage, and it made me realize how strong a person I was. I realized that I did not get my strong will from my mother.

Chapter 10: Past Secrets

As I was out on my daily walk, I started to think about secrets and how hard it was to keep them. I then thought about the big secret I had while growing up. I realized at an early age I was different. I was gay.

Growing up is hard enough. To be keeping this secret was very hard. I never came right out and told anyone in my family. We didn't have that comfortable talking communication relationship where I felt I could share this information. Boy, would it have made my life easier if I could have.

Here again was a case of secrets and not being myself. I recall bringing girlfriends to family get-togethers only to say, "This is my friend." My brother could say when we met a new girl he was dating, "This is my girlfriend." He was happy to explain how they met. I would make up a story of how my girlfriend and I knew each other through another friend. I didn't want to say "I met her at a gay bar." My parents must have noticed that after I graduated from high school, I had no boyfriends.

When I was eighteen years old, I was still living with my parents. I was outside cutting grass on the riding mower. Suddenly, I saw my mother walking with great determination toward me. She gestured for me to turn off the lawn mower, and I turned it off.

She said to me, "You know that bar you go to, well, something bad happened there last night. You better be careful going there." She then walked away. Not another word.

I remember sitting there in shock. Did my mother mention a gay bar to me? Does she know? Did the news flash on and say, "A local gay bar?" I finished cutting the grass in a bit of a fog. I realized that was her way of saying, I know. Make a point, and the conversation ended.

No one said anything about my being gay again for many years. Then, when my being gay was mentioned, no one even cared. That was my family's way of communicating.

When I was in high school, I dated one guy for about three-to-four years. He told Lucy and my other siblings: "I am going to be your brother-in-law one day." Lucy still laughs at that. She didn't believe him and probably knew I was gay and that my marriage to this guy was not going to happen.

Even minor things were difficult when I was growing up gay. I had to keep my being gay a secret because I feared being judged and rejected. As a gay person, you know you are different and worry that others will judge you. Surviving youth is hard, but being gay added more stress. I didn't want to date guys like my friends or cousins. I had to go out to meet women at gay bars. Everyone knows at least one person who is gay, but often that individual will stay under the radar and never come out and admit it due to this fear of being judged and rejected.

My parents never really asked anything about my girlfriends, neither did my siblings. They only asked years later after everyone knew I was gay. They did not ask about them when I was dating. Again, there was a lack of communication.

Once in a while now, my father will ask me, what happened to one of my old girlfriends? Do we still stay in touch? My parents and siblings liked some of the women I dated. My brother Greg, before he realized I was gay, said, "You have some cute girlfriends, are any of them single?" I just laughed.

When I was growing up, many individuals negatively judged gay people, and some still do. The attitude toward people with different sexual orientations has gotten a lot better with time. Never in my lifetime did I think gay marriage would pass. I always thought

I would be dead when this law passed. I guess that is how some women felt years ago when they couldn't vote.

Now, we look at the right of women to vote, and it is hard to believe that less than one hundred years ago, women were not allowed to vote. Many other things have changed a lot over time, including both the legality and increasing number of interracial marriages. The world is still going on, and none of these things has caused havoc, as some would have wanted us to think. But, we still do live in a world full of prejudice.

When the Supreme Court was deciding on the legality of the Defense of Marriage Act (DOMA), I was in a pension crisis over the beneficiary listed on my retirement pension. I had listed my partner even though we were not married. We owned a home, had joint bank accounts, life insurance, and shared financial responsibilities. We shared dogs and had our version of child care for our pets. I put her on my pension because if I died, I did not want her stuck with a mortgage that she couldn't pay, which was the way I could protect her. We lived just like a married couple, but legally because we were gay, we could not marry. After thirteen years, we went our separate ways, which was just like a divorce.

After we split, I wanted to remove my ex-partner's name as the contingent annuitant from my monthly pension check. This would stop my prior employer from taking the monthly deduction for having listing a beneficiary. If you had listed at your retirement a contingent annuitant, they take money out of each monthly paycheck. This allows you to have a percentage of your monthly pension check go to someone in the case of your death. As most people list their spouses, I listed my domestic partner. When I went to remove her name, my prior employer told me you could only remove a contingent annuitant if you divorced or the beneficiary dies.

I tried explaining that my beneficiary and I were NOT married. Gay marriage was not legal in our state. Since we were NOT married, we could NOT divorce. My ex-domestic partner was still alive. I simply wanted to remove her name as my beneficiary. I could not do so because of administrative legalese. I thought that if something happened to me, or if I died, my ex-partner would get my pension, not my family. This result did not seem right or even fair.

Changing my beneficiary seemed like a simple thing, but the law that prevented me from doing so was completely ridiculous. I don't think people who were writing contracts then considered the big picture. I hired an attorney to help me, but the cost was too much for me to continue my battle. I know others who were retired and had listed their domestic partners as beneficiaries. So, my problem was bound to happen to someone else.

While I was fighting this battle, the U.S. Supreme Court was hearing testimony about DOMA. DOMA was a federal law that said marriage could only be between a man and a woman, and that prohibited married same-sex couples from collecting federal benefits. I wrote many letters to politicians and anyone who would listen about my dilemma and the need to overturn DOMA. After I read Supreme Court Justice Sonia Sotomayor's book *My Beloved World,* I thought: what an incredible woman she is. Reading her book made me want to keep fighting this issue. She was determined to get where she is, and I am, too. I wrote to her, but I never received a response. I hope she read my letter, and it helped her make her decision regarding the Defense of Marriage Act.

Finally, on June 26, 2015, DOMA was overruled by the U.S. Supreme Court decision in *Obergefell v. Hodges.* This ruling was vitally important to me because my prior employer told me that the only way I could remove my ex's name was if DOMA was ruled unconstitutional. When the Supreme Court overturned the Defense of Marriage Act, gay marriage became legal. I could get married to someone else and remove my ex-partner's name and substitute my wife's name.

I kept thinking, how would a straight, divorced couple feel if one person died and the divorced living spouse would get the pension of their former spouse? This situation made no sense to me. Gay couples still do not have enough protection. There are still many state rules that restrict their rights. Many rules still need to change.

Being able to be married definitely has helped. However, we still had to make sure we had everything in order before we could get married. We had our wills, homes in both names; everything was held jointly so no one could take away something that wasn't theirs. Since we were domestic partners, all our financial stuff had to be in order, including designation of beneficiaries. We had no legal rights as married couples do. Married couples did not have to worry about such details.

Because we lived in Maryland, a state that has equal rights, we did not have to worry about many of the problems that gay people have in other states. Having equal rights is why we live in Maryland. In some states, gay people are still fighting court battles over DOMA legislation regarding payment of income taxes and other benefits for same-sex married couples.

For example, some gay people still have to worry about people refusing to serve them because they are gay. In early 2017, there was a trial piece of legislation in the Oval Office to restrict the rights of gays. The president has said that he would not sign it at this time, but this means he might approve it at another time. We still need to have everything in order in case someone would come along and try to take away our equal rights. That will always be in the back of our minds. It's sad that we still have to hold onto this worry. There is still hatred in this country. After the overturn of the Defense of Marriage Act, my pension issue disappeared only after Laurie and I were married.

Once we legally married in our state, my prior employer removed my ex-partner's name, and my wife, Laurie, was listed. All the money I spent on attorney fees still makes me upset. I couldn't believe all of this was happening. Never in my life did I think the day would come when I could be married to my wife, Laurie. We have been together about eight years, including four as a married couple. I wouldn't change a thing. I am happier than I ever thought I could be. Yes, Laurie now can get my pension, as it should be.

That fight ended, but as I said before, gay couples still need more protections. Anti-hate laws and anti-discrimination laws for gay couples should be nationwide. Our protection should not be based on what state in which we choose to live. That, in itself, divides people. Everyone throughout our nation should receive protection.

Now, I faced another big fight for the truth about my paternity.

Chapter 11: Paternity

Who is my biological father? Lucy and I were talking and thinking more about this. Was James, my mother's old friend, my biological father? Could this be? Where do I start?

I decided to try to find James's son Keith on Facebook. I know a little about Keith, because of things my mother has told me over the years. Now, I needed to search for him and tell him what has happened with my DNA results. I found him fairly quickly. I sent him a private message on Facebook without too much detail. I asked him to call me as soon as he could.

Keith called fairly quickly. I explained to him who I was and asked if he knew or remembered my mother. He said he not only remembered my mother, but he liked her.

I told Keith about my DNA results and the possibility that he and I could be half-siblings. He didn't seem too shocked. However, he told me that his father, James, had passed away in 2013.

I told Keith that my mother had emailed me his father's obituary. I explained that when I received it, I thought it was strange that she was sending it to me. I wondered, could she have sent it because she knew he was my father? And, if he were my biological father, I would be upset that I didn't find this out sooner.

Keith told me that when he was a teenager, he realized that his father and my mother probably were having an affair. He remembered going to my mother's office with his father to visit her. He said his father made model ships, and he saw them in my mother's office. He thought at the time; they must be good friends for her to have some of his father's model ships. Keith's father, James, was also married at this time.

Keith understood the situation and agreed to send away for an Ancestry.com DNA kit for himself. He wanted to know if I was his half-sister. I thanked Keith, and he promised to let me know as soon as his results were available. He joked and said, "If we are related, I guess you will see the results probably before me on Ancestry.com." We exchanged email addresses and said goodbye.

Chapter 12: I Need a Psychic

A few days after receiving my DNA news about my father, I decided I would get a reading from a psychic I had seen before, Dr. Gee. She was in a small town in Maryland. The first time I saw her, I had a very good experience. Dr. Gee was right on point about things in my life. She told me details about life events that would happen, and, in fact, they did occur.

I wish years ago she would have foreseen the DNA issues that were happening in my life. But, I guess figuring out this path is my life's journey now. I can't change things.

I did not know how my reading would go with Dr. Gee, but I was excited to see her. As I arrived in her office, I had a list of questions. Dr. Gee always tells you to bring a list of questions. I asked several questions about my biological father, hoping I could get some clear answers, to help guide me in my search.

Dr. Gee told me the first letter of my biological father's last name. She said his first name had an "A" sound in it, and he was still living. She listed several states connected with him. I was happy he was still living. At least, there was a possibility that I could meet him.

Dr. Gee gave me a lot of information, and now I needed to think and process this information. Everything happened so quickly in the reading, and I didn't want to forget anything, so I recorded the session. I couldn't wait to get home and listen to my session. Sometimes, when you write notes, you may lose some of the things people say. It's easier to record the session, and doing so keeps you focused. In fact, Dr. Gee encourages those for whom she reads to record these sessions.

On my way home, I kept thinking about everything she said in my reading. Dr. Gee told me that my biological father was still living, but she claimed that he did not know about me. Was this true? Did my mother keep this secret from him and me? If my mother kept this secret from him, I would be angry. She kept secrets from Lucy and me. What about our other siblings? I don't understand this secret-keeping.

Going to see a psychic is part of my belief in the spiritual world. I believe there are many levels of the spiritual world, and people can get closer to a deeper understanding through energy work, reiki, massage, and many other things that can be beneficial to us. Yes, I do believe in the afterlife and ghosts. I have surrounded myself with many friends who also share beliefs in the spiritual world. The power of healing is very much alive.

I think having this frame of mind makes me strong-willed and keeps me positive about all the things happening in my life. Still, I can be shocked and overwhelmed, but it does not keep me from moving on and having a good life.

Sometimes, when situations, such as the current one, become overpowering, I need to take time away and center myself. I need to rev up my energy levels to get back on track. After all of the stress of the last year, I have learned to meditate and am involved with reiki and energy work. I also have learned that meditation is something I can do daily on my own. I enjoy listening to the track "Healing Meditation" on the CD *Regression to Time and Places*, by Brian L Weiss, M.D. It keeps me feeling grounded and at peace and gets me ready to start a new day, like getting a charge on my battery.

Similarly, reiki and energy work help keep me at peace. My friend Leslie N. Bank, a former Baltimore police lieutenant and security consultant, wrote the book *The Receptivity Project: Make the Connection* (2015, CreateSpace), where she explains how to balance your energy and your spiritual body. She urges us to trust our intuition from the spirit world—our gut instincts and funny feelings. I found this is a great explanation of what we all are capable of doing.

These revelations are happening to teach me a life lesson that I need to learn. I don't know what this lesson is or why it is occurring now, but I strongly believe we are all put on earth to learn lessons. Maybe I did something in a past life to be here now and learn this lesson.

Chapter 13: Wrong Information

Weeks went by quickly. I spent much time researching on Ancestry.com for the answers. I looked at all the DNA hits that connected to me and compared them with others.

I realized while searching for Lucy's father that some people put the wrong information in their family trees. Some of these individuals might not have undergone DNA testing and don't know who their biological parents are or they simply listed the information others told them in the tree. This information is not always correct. DNA was changing my tree.

Think of all the books on family genealogy: who belonged where, whose kids were whose. No one had to provide DNA to write their family history. Years ago, did the authors of these genealogies do DNA tests to prove their heritage? Of course not. DNA testing did not even get started until the 1986 DNA profiling. Your parents and grandparents told you about your family.

Many individuals backed up their oral histories with documents to prove their claims. But, now, DNA was proving some of these stories were wrong. No one took into consideration affairs that were happening. DNA testing is changing history for many, not just in their genealogy but as a practical matter in what they know about themselves. What people told us about our family and even ourselves might have been stories based on wishful thinking and not on reality.

I now have to change my family tree to list an unknown father. That changes my whole history as I knew it. I also needed to change Lucy's paternity to show Robert as her father, a change of history for her.

Additionally, some people copy other people's family trees and don't bother to gather their facts or verify the facts that they copy. To make an accurate family tree, you have to take the time to research and document every detail. Such specificity requires that you look at everything: death certificates, wills, census information, anything that will verify what you think you know. Then, you can put the correct information in your family tree.

Even though I learned the basics of researching on Ancestry.com fairly quickly, I knew I needed help researching, so I reached out to my childhood friend Janet. Janet is like a little sister to me. She has been working on her family genealogy for years. She knows a lot more about Ancestry.com and searching than I do.

I first told Janet about Lucy; then, I told her my DNA story. Janet was a bit shocked. She knows my entire family. We were neighbors as children, and all our siblings have grown up together. She now knows our family secrets.

We joked and said such goings on must have resulted from "something in the water." In our old neighborhood, we were aware of other crazy things that happened with families. We had two neighbors who were having an affair. Then, we discovered that their spouses also were having affairs. It was our little soap opera.

As kids, while we played, we saw parents doing things that they had no idea we saw or heard. We saw parents exchanging kisses with people other than their spouse when they did not think anyone was looking. All we can do now is laugh about it.

Janet agreed to help me solve the mystery, about who my biological father was. My mother was not helping much, so I needed Janet's help. I am grateful for her help. As we chatted on the phone, we started constructing my new family tree.

I wanted to title the tree, "Who's your daddy?" I did not do that, if you were wondering. I do have a funny sense of humor and will keep making fun of this in spite of its serious nature. That is just me.

Chapter 14: A New Tree and My Mother's Parkinson's

As I began, I hoped my search would be as easy as it was to find Lucy's father. As the search continued, I realized that my search would be difficult and require a lot of patience and detective work. Being an investigator was part of my prior career, so I considered myself perfect for this job.

Janet and I had a lot of DNA matches to compare. Ancestry.com showed hundreds of DNA connections for me, and I realized that going through them would take some time. First, I wanted to look at the closest DNA connections to see with whom they shared DNA. This task was a bit overwhelming. We had to pull out my matches with Lucy since we now know that we have different fathers. Purging our matches allowed us to eliminate the matches that we shared with our mother's DNA.

Every few days, I questioned my mother in person or over the phone. I kept asking her, "Who is my father?" Did she not remember who my father was? Was this part of her illness? Or was she just lying to me to keep her secret? I am shocked that she was not giving me the answer I wanted.

While I was conducting this research online, I read John Bradshaw's best-known book *Family Secrets: The Path from Shame to Healing* (1995, Bantam Books). He recounted the story of a woman named Mary Sue who kept the knowledge of her son's paternity from him, and as a result, he was furious; he cut her off emotionally and refused to speak to her. By keeping her dark secret, she could never heal her guilt and dishonesty. The secret prevented her from the possibility of ever receiving forgiveness and reconciliation with her family. I wondered whether this would be my mother's fate.

After several weeks, for my sanity, I decided that I needed to stop calling my mother. She finally started calling me to check in. I don't think she liked when I did not speak to her. When I finally spoke to her, she started asking me crazy questions such as, "How is your research going looking for your biological father?" I said to her, "How about you just tell me the truth and provide some answers." My mother's questions were not something I wanted to hear and, in fact, they shocked me. I did not want to be mean to my mother, but she was frustrating me. I was not willing to play a game with her.

Despite all the tension, I am thankful I still have my sense of humor. It's my nature to laugh. I think if my personality were different, all of this would have crushed me. Instead, I sat back and laughed. Maybe a psychologist would say that I needed therapy. My response would be to tell those interested: "My therapy is to talk about this and write a book." It is not my style to keep things bottled up inside.

My parents were not the best communicators, as I have said before. I believe it was the way their parents raised them. They did not know how to discuss personal issues.

My wife and I joke all the time that my way of communicating is not like theirs. My wife would tease me—are you even from this family? By contrast with my parents, my wife and I constantly talk about things that occur and things that bother us. We express our feelings and welcome each other's input. Such behavior is not something I practiced while I was growing up. I am not sure why I am the total opposite of my parents. Maybe my friends and my career changed me. In my prior career, I needed to talk and get answers all the time.

When I was growing up, if you had an issue, the last person you talked to were your parents. You would tell your friends. Now, as an adult, looking back at my childhood, I wish communication would have been better within our family.

I wish my parents would have talked to us in a way that most families communicate. I remember my father's best friend, his family, and kids. They always seemed to share their problems and sat down as a family to figure things out. That never happened in our family. I think my parents would ignore many issues. My parents seemed to tiptoe around anything personal. They must have thought that maybe these issues would disappear if they didn't talk about them.

For example, if someone died, they would say something in casual conversation days later. They never asked how my siblings or I felt, and they never asked if we were okay. If they didn't talk about it, it was as if it never happened.

Despite the behavior toward my siblings, my parents were very loving toward me. Lucy might say they weren't that way with her. I never saw the side of my parents that Lucy did. As I previously noted, the age difference between us must have played a role.

As I indicated earlier, my mother suffered from numerous health issues. Until now she never said she had Parkinson's disease. She was once a very strong woman but has become quite fragile. It is hard to watch your parents go through any disease, but Parkinson's is among the worst. I watched the changing of her body into this frail person. She seemed to age overnight.

I first noticed my mother's thumb twitching years ago. She would try to hide the movement by covering up one hand with the other hand. My wife and I had discussed my mother's thumb twitching many times after seeing her. My wife has been an operating room nurse for almost thirty years. She told me about the tremors and balance issues Parkinson's could cause. I told my mother that I thought she should go to a neurologist because I thought she was showing symptoms of Parkinson's disease.

My mother, of course, didn't listen to me. She chose to ignore the problem as always, by not talking about it. A few years passed and she eventually went to the doctor. The doctor diagnosed her with Parkinson's disease. Parkinson's disease is a disorder of the nervous system that affects movement. It is a hard disease to watch anyone go through. There are tremors, balance issues, and stiffness of the body.

There is no cure for this disease. Medicine seems to help the tremors, but the ravages of the disease were slowly wearing my mother down. Her balance was terrible, and I waited for that phone call from my father that she had fallen and hurt herself.

My mother used to be a very active person. She travelled widely. She painted the inside of her entire house when she was sixty-five years old. She had a lot of energy. When doctors finally diagnosed the disease, it was as though she had aged twenty years. She chose to be inactive and not help herself. It is sad to watch.

She also has major forgetfulness and an "I don't care attitude." Spending time with her has made me reevaluate my own life. I am hoping Parkinson's doesn't happen to me or anyone else who I love. I started reading about Parkinson's disease so I could understand what was happening to my mother's health. I have tried to explain it as best I can to my father so he can understand why my mother's habits have changed. Her movement and balance issues are more severe now. Sometimes, I saw my father getting frustrated that my mother doesn't move around as he does. He never talked about it unless I started a conversation. Once again, the family trait of non-communication endured.

Parkinson's disease has affected many people, including former U.S. Attorney General Janet Reno. She died of complications from Parkinson's disease at age seventy-eight.

Unlike my mother, Janet Reno did not let the disease define her. I will always remember her as a strong woman, who stood up for human rights.

Another famous person who has Parkinson's disease is the actor Michael J. Fox (1961-). He was diagnosed with young-onset Parkinson's disease in 1991 when he was only twenty-nine years old. The Michael J. Fox foundation for Parkinson's Research (https://www.michaeljfox.org) offers much useful information for understanding the disease and staying on top of the latest research. I hope people will continue to work with this foundation to find a cure.

According to studies, the cause of the disease is unknown. However, advancing age is the single biggest risk factor for Parkinson's disease. Some forms are hereditary. I often wondered about my risks of getting this disease. My mother and her brother both have the disease. As a kid, some of my great-aunts on my mother's side of the family would shake and have tremors. The disease, which usually chooses one gender over another, did not choose gender in my family.

Like many diseases, I can only hope researchers will discover a cure for my mother and others who are suffering. Even though Parkinson's is hereditary, I hope that I didn't get these genes and that the genes from my father, whoever he is, will be free of major hereditary diseases.

I kept telling myself that I needed to understand why my mother was not giving me the facts. Why wasn't she responding? Was it because she couldn't remember, and was this part of the disease? Her behavior was not an easy thing to understand, but if her elusive answers were part of her disease, I can't allow myself to stay angry at her. Parkinson's causes thinking difficulties, and I see it causing some dementia in my mother. Can she not remember her past?

I have had a few doctor's appointments recently, and it felt weird telling the doctor, I did not know the answers to some of her questions. Now, I don't know what diseases run on my father's side of the family. I don't even know who my father is, and this lack of knowledge about my paternity was not something I ever thought I would be saying to a doctor or anyone else.

I felt embarrassed telling someone I did not know who my father was. I don't know why I felt this way. Maybe it was the fact that it made my mother look bad or maybe I felt judged. I felt judged enough growing up gay. The ambiguity about who my father was brought back those judgmental feelings. When I thought about it, I considered times when I heard others say they didn't know a parent. It made me feel sad for that person. Now, I felt sad for myself and a little numb.

As a child, I was sad for kids who didn't know their parents for whatever reason. I think children are sensitive to that situation because they look up to their parents and find it hard to imagine not having their parents around.

If someone were adopted or had step-parents, it seemed different to us who had two biological parents. When the mother of a classmate committed suicide, all the kids in school were quiet because they did not know what to say or do. I still think about this classmate from time to time and wonder how he is on Mother's Day. What an awful thing to experience as a child.

As I mentioned, I never questioned who my parents were. I wonder how I would have felt as a child if I had known the father who raised me was not my biological father. What would I have done differently?

Chapter 15: Thanksgiving

When Thanksgiving came around, I knew it was going to be an interesting day for us. My entire family was at Lucy's house. Since Lucy and I know all these secrets, I was sure it would be a strange day.

As we sat around eating dinner and chatting, Lucy and I were waiting for our niece Carol to say something to her grandfather about the family. For example, she might have asked, "What are you thankful for?" If she had asked this or some other topic, it might have led to a conversation about Lucy's paternity. Carol is one of those people, like me, who needed to know everything that was going on. Our niece Carol suspected that Lucy had another father. She heard this rumor years ago, from her mother, Denise, our sister.

Carol began getting interested in genealogy and was putting together a database so she would understand more about our family. She was at my house looking at genealogy documents when we found the love letter my father had written to my mother. I'm sure she discussed this with her mother, my sister Denise.

Carol didn't know her grandfather has already admitted the truth to Lucy. She didn't know anything about what had already happened. Lucy and I have not told anyone in our family, only our spouses and a few close friends.

We waited apprehensively, anticipating what someone might say at the dinner table. Maybe our father would say something. It was a quiet dinner. I wondered whether my father thought that everyone in this room knew he admitted not being Lucy's father.

In fact, only a few of us knew the truth, and we were not telling anyone yet. I am sure my father was feeling awkward. Lucy still had said nothing to him about the letter he wrote her admitting the truth of her paternity.

He admitted he was not her father, but Lucy would not talk to him about it. Since our parents did not know how to communicate, they did not teach us this skill. So, it was hard for us to talk to them. Then, the awkwardness of this letter overshadowed the whole dinner. Lucy and I were giggling a bit waiting for it all to explode. It was Thanksgiving, and things always seem to happen at family gatherings.

Our mother just sat there in silence eating dinner, acting as if nothing had happened. Finally, our parents and Greg left Lucy's house. Now, Lucy and I were able to chat quietly about what had been going on. We both were still surprised that our niece Carol did not say anything to our father. We were thankful that it ended up being a quiet day.

Chapter 16: Is This the Answer?

Weeks after Thanksgiving, Janet and I were still researching family trees. We would spend hours sitting in front of the computer. It seemed all my free time was on the computer seeking the answer. I felt as if my eyeballs were going to pop out of my head after staring at the computer screen so long.

On a Sunday afternoon, my wife suggested we go to lunch at one of our favorite Mexican restaurants and visit my parents. She thought she could distract my father long enough for me to have another conversation with my mother. Of course, I wanted to go to lunch. I wasn't very excited about going to my parents', after staring at the computer for weeks trying to get the answers. I really didn't want to talk to my mother. I knew I needed answers, but I was not in the mood for her non-communication.

However, after lunch, we headed over to my parents' house for a drop-in visit. When we arrived, my mother took me into her room to show me something. We were alone now, and it gave us the opportunity to talk.

My wife and my father were watching the playoff game for the Super Bowl on television—the perfect distraction. I had so much on my mind that I didn't even know who was playing in the playoff games for the Super Bowl championship.

After we reached my mother's room, she started to show me a photo album of certificates she had received while working for the government. Out of nowhere, she suddenly told me to write down a name. I immediately looked for paper and a pen. I didn't want her to forget or change her thought process.

She provided me with a man's first name and spelled it differently than I thought someone would spell it. I questioned her about the spelling. She told me that her spelling was right. She was very direct about how to spell the name. I wrote it down. Then, she told me the last name. She also spelled the last name for me. I wrote down everything she told me, including details about where this man lived and his family.

I wondered if these were clues. Was my mother now telling me directly who my biological father was? I was stunned but happy that she was giving me a name. Maybe one day I can get the whole truth. I wondered if this could be that day. I hoped so.

I was a little cautious because of all the prior conversations. I didn't know what I believed. My mother would tell me one thing one day, and the next week something else. My mother's health issues caused her memory to be better on some days, and not so good on other days. I thought this might be a good day.

I am thankful that my wife had a gut feeling to go to my parents' house. My mother seemed very focused this day—a good day for her, and I hoped this meant good information for me.

As I thought about the name she had given me, I realized that it was the same information that the psychic, Dr. Gee, had told me a few weeks back. The initial was correct for his last name, and there was an "A" sound in this man's first name. Was this the answer? Did my mother tell me his name for real? Was Dr. Gee again correct in providing me information?

As soon as my wife and I got in the car, I asked her to search the name my mother had just given me. "Dr. Gee gave me the same last name initial for my biological father," I explained.

She searched the Internet and found a possible match fairly quickly. She started reading the information as soon as I drove out of their driveway. However, she became carsick from reading while in the moving car. She told me: "We'll need to wait until we get home. Then, we can start reading about this complete stranger—who could or could not be your biological father."

All the way home, I wondered—did my mother give me a good name? I kept thinking: why would she give me someone's name if it were not true? She knew I would try to contact him and the family. Would she have given me false information? What did she have to lose if I knew the truth?

I simply wanted the truth and wanted to get my health history. Of course, I would like to know who this man was. I assured my mother many times over that I would not tell my father he was not my father. It sounded stupid to even say it to myself—my father is not my father.

No matter what the DNA shows, I will still consider him my father. I thought of all the things I did in documenting genealogy on his side of the family. Now, that was not even my family's genealogy.

I was attached to another whole family. Perhaps I had other siblings. The thought of having other relatives continued to shock me. Did I miss out on knowing this whole other group?

It made me sad to think my "granny" wasn't really my granny. I now say she was my "play" granny. "Play" is the way I refer to anyone who wasn't a blood relative anymore. Now, I had lots of "play" cousins and "play" uncles and "play" aunts. I had to see some humor in all of this, since I can't change it.

I even needed to laugh to myself a little after I saw my father and he commented that "You better hope you don't get my ailment." He always referred to things being hereditary. "You better hope you don't get what I have when you get older." His mother, "granny," or his father had some ailments that could be hereditary, he told me.

Keeping the secret of my paternity from my father is difficult. When he talks about hereditary ailments, I can't tell him not to worry. I can't tell him that I won't get what's in his genes.

Instead, I just listen to him, and I agree. It made me a little sad. I felt conflicted about not being straight with him.

As soon as my wife and I got home, we started searching the Internet. We found the same man as we did in the car. When checking Facebook, we found him and possibly family members. We found pictures on the Internet of someone by his name, but was this person my father?

We still did not know for sure if it was him. All the clues were saying yes, but my doubt was still there. My mother had given me very detailed information, which fit perfectly with this man. We then realized some of his family, including his children, live or lived near where I grew up.

What were the chances that we found him so quickly? While I was in our home office looking at the information on the computer, I wondered if I should call him. If I did call him, what would I say? I did not know what to do.

I kept wondering, did my mother give me the correct information? I didn't want to rattle someone's world if what she told me was not true. But, the facts were there from my mother, they had an affair. Could this man be my biological father?

I decided to search Ancestry.com for all my DNA results. I would put his last name in my search field. I could see if anyone with his surname had done a DNA test and if it would be a match to me. I put his name into the search field, and a match to his surname appeared. I needed to connect the dots and figure out this piece of the puzzle. I needed my friend Janet's help on the Ancestry.com website now more than ever. I contacted Janet, and with both of us searching, I thought maybe we would be able to find the answer.

After thinking about how to contact my potential biological father for a few days, I decided to send a private message through Messenger directly to this man. Let's call him "Billy." What did I have to lose? After all, Billy could be my biological father. Maybe he would want to know, or perhaps he knew already?

A few days had elapsed since I sent Billy a private message, but I had not heard anything from him. Did he get my message? I had left my email and phone number. At this point, I felt quite confused and wondered what I should do now, since he had not responded.

I decided to send a message to Lisa, who I thought was one of Billy's grandchildren. I realized that one of my friends on Facebook might be friends with this Lisa. What were the chances of that? We sometimes say that it's a small world, but this was making my world seem quite condensed.

I sent this Lisa a private message through Facebook. I asked if she were, in fact, a granddaughter of Billy. Lisa responded right away. "Yes, that's my grandfather," she said.

My heart was pounding. I was not sure what to do, or what to tell Lisa. Finally, I decided I would tell her in a message that Billy was an old friend of my mother's, and I was trying to contact him. I asked if she would get a message to him to contact me. I explained that I had sent him a private message through Facebook, but I did not know if he had received it.

I realized that some people don't pay attention to Facebook Messenger. I found I even had an old message on my Messenger that I did not see for about a year. Now, I was more aware of this feature.

Perhaps Billy didn't see my message. I knew my father was not good at the computer. Maybe Billy, who probably was about the same age, was the same way.

Lisa sent me another message and said Billy would be in town for the Christmas holidays. He would be staying in town until the New Year. She agreed to give him my message.

I thanked her. Now, I had to wait. It was weird to think that Billy was coming into town, and could be close to where I lived for several weeks.

Was this an opportunity to meet him? How was this supposed to work? When he found out I was trying to reach him, would he know why? Did he know I exist? How would he act? Lots of thoughts were going through my head.

My mother claimed that Billy did not know about me. Was she telling the truth? My mother's statement gave me a strange feeling. I could never imagine having a child out there and not knowing about that child.

My mother told me Billy was married and had six children. If he were my biological father, that means I have a lot more siblings. Well, more half-siblings.

I started to think: did I have any full siblings? My head was spinning due to all these potential facts now having an impact on my life. I was fifty years old and finding this out. Lucy, Denise, and Greg were now my half-siblings? Six more half-siblings out there? I had many emotions to process.

Something new was happening every day. Sometimes, it felt a bit crazy and overwhelming. But, I always managed to smile. That's just me.

Thankfully, my wife was a great listener. She kept me calm and helped put everything in perspective. She aided me in finding humor in all of this. I would be lost without her.

Now I needed Lisa's help; I still had not heard anything from Billy. Christmas was getting closer. I decided to send another message to Lisa. This time in my message on Facebook Messenger, I sent my cell phone number and asked her to call me. I explained that I still had not heard anything from Billy, and it was very important that I talk with him.

I didn't know what else to do. I figured, Lisa was young and thus, she would be more open. Would she be okay with all of this? After all, she could be my niece.

Hours passed, and I still had not heard anything from Lisa. I felt a bit anxious. I decided the next thing I should do was to send Lisa's mother a message through Messenger.

Looking at Facebook, I was able to determine who was who in this family. I found Lisa's mother, Mari. I sent Mari a private message on Messenger and asked her to call me. I explained that I needed to tell her something. I did not want to put the information on Messenger, so I gave her my cell number. I did not even know if she would get my message.

Now, I had three messages out there to these people I didn't know—one to Billy, one to Lisa, and the other to Mari. At this stage, I needed to have patience, keep calm, and wait. Late that night, Lisa sent me a text message, but I was already sleeping. My phone was off. Her message said she would call me the next day after work. She explained that she had been out of town and had just gotten home.

After reading the text on my phone, I felt a little better. I knew at least Lisa wasn't ignoring my message. I realized it was going to be a long day as I waited for her call.

Chapter 17: The First Conversation

When the phone rang, it was Lisa. I poured a glass of wine to calm my nerves. I didn't even know Lisa, but this whole situation was making me a bit nervous. I guess I had a right to be nervous. Wine was perfect for calming my nerves. It was a "heavy pour."

I told Lisa when she called, that according to my mother, her grandfather and my mother had an affair for many years. As a result, I believed her grandfather could be my biological father.

I explained about my DNA test and the possible connection to her family. I related the conversations I had with my mother about her grandfather. Lisa explained that she had a gut feeling that maybe this was what I wanted to tell her.

She joked with me and told me she stuck her foot in her mouth, not meaning to do so. She left a voice message for Billy on his answering machine telling him I was trying to reach him because he knew my mother. She jokingly asked if my mother were his mistress.

We laughed a little about that, trying to make some humor out of the situation. Humor is always the best medicine. We talked for more than an hour, during which Lisa told me a little about her family. I told her about mine.

She did not want any of this to hurt her grandmother. I told her that I did not either. I explained that I could not tell my father he was not my biological father because I did not want to hurt him either.

We discussed her doing a DNA test to determine if we were related. We hoped that this would help us get some answers. I explained to Lisa that I sent her mother, Mari, a private message on Messenger and asked her to call me. I did not know what to do in this situation, so I had reached out to both of them.

Lisa told me that she wanted to think about all of this. She asked me not to answer my phone if her mother, Mari, called. She wanted a chance to talk to her mother first. She did not know how her mother would react. I agreed that I would wait.

Her mother got my message and called me fairly quickly. I let my phone go to voicemail since I told Lisa that I would wait for her to talk to Mari first. I didn't want to break my promise.

This situation seemed crazy. I was waiting for a potential "niece" I did not know, to let me know when it would be okay for me to talk to my potential "half-sister."

I had always felt as if my life were a *Seinfeld* television episode filled with crazy things that happened. For example, I was in a grocery store using the self-checkout. Of course, the machine ran out of money, and I could not get the change I was due. I was in a hurry, and the cashier who was supposed to be around to help with problems was not there. So, when someone finally showed up, I told them "You know how to take my money, you just don't know how to give me my change."

My situation in the grocery store reminded me of the *Seinfeld* episode when Jerry was trying to get a rental car, and they didn't have his car. He said: "You know how to make the reservation, you just can't keep the reservation." The *Seinfeld* situation was similar to what happened to me at the store; they took my money but could not give me my change.

I watched another *Seinfeld* episode recently. Jerry was eating a black and white cookie. He felt ill and talked about how he had not thrown up since 1980, and his long streak without throwing up was about to be broken. Again, the *Seinfeld* episode was just like me. I have not thrown up since 1987, and I had a long streak going. I remembered exactly why and where I was when it last happened.

I had just gotten my heart broken by a girlfriend. I went out
on a date with a new girl, and she went to kiss me at the end of the
date. As she leaned in to kiss me, I said goodnight and ran into my
apartment. I knew what was coming—throw-up time. That should
have been my first clue about this woman, not good news. Later, I
realized my girlfriend broke my heart, and I was not ready for
dating. My body was sending me a message.

Part of the way I keep my good humor intact is by finding
something funny I can relate to in the television show. I seem to be
able to quote many lines, as I am sure many people can, which is
why the program has had such success over many years, and people
never get tired of watching the reruns.

Now, I can add this funny, weird encounter with this family.
The sad thing is that I almost felt as if I were doing something
wrong. I was telling this big secret. I believed I was doing the right
thing. Secrets will come out; they always do. Knowledge about my
paternity was a big secret, but I decided that I would not keep it—
except perhaps from my dad.

Early the next morning, my phone rang. Mari was calling,
Lisa was now okay with me speaking to her. Mari and I talked for
more than an hour. She also suspected what I was going to tell her
and did not seem shocked. We talked about her family and mine. It
was a pleasant conversation. She made me feel at ease.

Ironically, two of her siblings went to high school with two
of my siblings, Lucy and Denise. Now, once again I saw that this is a
small world.

I realized while talking with Mari that I had things in
common with her and Billy. She told me that Billy helps out in
cemeteries working with veterans' families. I spend time in
cemeteries documenting graves. I have been involved with the

85

county where I live, helping to document old graves to try and preserve the cemeteries and keep them from being destroyed.

The county wants to document all the graves on public or private property to protect them. We, the volunteers, documented their locations. Based on the county records of many of their locations, we went out and searched for the actual tombstones. Some citizens had called the county when this project started to report that there were graves on their property after they read about the project in the newspaper. Billy and I both seemed to have an interest in cemeteries. I felt we had much more in common. My background was in investigation; his background included a secret position with the military, according to his daughter.

Nevertheless, I needed Billy to get a DNA test to prove he was my biological father—that was all I wanted right now.

Mari told me that while Billy was in town from Florida for the holidays, she was going to pull him aside and ask him about my mother, and then tell him about me. I agreed and told her I thought that was a good idea. Now, I had to wait until she confronted him. Weeks went by before Mari called me back. My nerves were on edge as I anxiously waited.

Chapter 18: The Confrontation

Mari called and told me that she confronted Billy. He denied I could be his daughter. I could not believe what I was hearing. He did not deny the affair with my mother, but he commented to Mari that he did not "ejaculate," so I can't be his daughter. What?

My first thought was, who says that word to his daughter? I could never imagine my father saying this to any of his kids. As Mari was telling me about their conversation, I was in shock—both by his denial and by his choice of words.

Now, I thought—he denied the possibility that he could be my biological father. He did not deny the affair. He denied that my mother could have gotten pregnant. The bottom line was that he did not say anything about wanting to do a DNA test.

I was in complete shock at this conversation and about what was happening. I wondered: Doesn't Billy want to know if I'm his daughter? Does he not care? Now, where do I go?

I refused to feel as if I had done something wrong. My mother and Billy had an affair. Billy and my mother were wrong for having an affair.

Mari told me that Lisa was ordering a DNA kit from Ancestry.com. They also wanted to know the truth. Lisa and I had discussed her doing a DNA test when we first talked.

I am grateful that Lisa was going to do the DNA test for me. I needed the answer. Now, I had to wait for the kit to be ordered, delivered, and the final result delivered. It seemed like it was a long time to wait. However, waiting seemed to be all I was doing these days.

With Christmas, almost here, I knew Ancestry.com would be busy with DNA kits, which meant that their matching would take longer than usual. I wished they could have ordered the kit sooner. I wanted the answers, and it was so hard to wait.

I hoped Mari would want to test her DNA instead of her daughter. This way, it would show a closer match. Billy was her father. However, I wasn't going to push the issue since they were paying for their own DNA kit. The kits with tax were usually a little more than one hundred dollars.

Christmas Eve arrived. Mari texted me wishing my family a Merry Christmas. That meant a lot to me. Her message let me know that she was thinking about all of this, and not thinking I was some crazy person out there making up stories. I wished her family a Merry Christmas back.

Meantime, while I waited for the answers from the DNA test, my friend Janet and I were busy on the computer. We both spent hours every day trying to find more DNA connections to Billy's family. We built a family tree from Billy's name. It went backwards to his parents, grandparents, great-great grandparents, and so on.

Building a family tree and searching for answers is quite a job. Janet was perfect for this job. She had been doing genealogy for many years with her own family. She knew all the ins and outs. I was lucky to have her help.

We found two, maybe three connections to Billy's family from my DNA matches. The first one, I matched to another person through Billy's fifth great-grandparent, eight generations back. We went back to the 1700s to 1800s to find these connections.

Janet was convinced that I was Billy's daughter based on the DNA connections we had found. I was more skeptical than she was. I needed to receive the confirmation of the DNA test—hard-concrete evidence.

Chapter 19: The Possible Half-Sibs Are Calling

While on the computer, working on the family tree in Ancestry.com, I received an email from someone named "Matt" in my Ancestry.com message box. He was one of my possible half-siblings. He asked me how I was related to the surname of his family. He must have seen my family tree.

Did Mari or Lisa tell him? Was this message him being sneaky, trying to find out about me? I needed to think how I should respond. I was tired of all the lies and decided that I was going to tell the truth.

Strange things had been happening. A few days earlier someone else sent me an email asking questions about my Ancestry.com tree and my relationship with the family. Was this a coincidence? Was something going on in this family to which I needed to pay more attention? Were they trying to figure out if I was related to them?

I had become suspicious of this whole situation. Did Billy, who did not think I was his daughter, put his son Matt up to get the answers? I found the timing of Matt contacting me very odd. Before I answered Matt, I decided to contact Lisa and explain that Matt had sent me an email about obtaining information. He was asking how I was related to their family.

Lisa told me that Matt was on Ancestry.com for a different reason. He saw a census report from 1940 on Billy's family and had been trying to make sense of it. Lisa thought he was innocently reaching out to me because I was researching their surname and had a family tree attached to their name.

I told Lisa that I was not going to lie to Matt. I was going to tell him that we could be related. She agreed that the lies needed to stop, and she told me she would contact her mother and tell her about Matt emailing me through Ancestry.com.

During our conversation, I asked Lisa if she had sent her DNA kit to Ancestry.com. She told me that she had not yet mailed it. She had gotten busy with the holidays and other things. She apologized and promised to do the test after work and mail it.

I was disappointed that she had not already done the test. I thought that we would have the results fairly soon. I was wrong. I was getting more agitated as the potential answer drew closer to me.

After I finished talking to Lisa, she sent pictures of her family to my cell phone. It was weird to think that the pictures I was seeing were possibly my half-siblings and my biological father.

When I looked at Billy's picture, I saw myself, and I saw myself in a few of his kids. Maybe I just imagined this. Maybe my brain was playing tricks on me, and I saw something that was not there. I did feel as if I were looking in the mirror when I looked at Billy. I got the same feeling as when I was looking at my mother's pictures because I saw family resemblances.

Seeing someone who looked like me made me feel odd. I have never thought I looked like the father who raised me. Now, I looked at Billy's picture and said to myself—that is my biological father. I do look like him. Was this just an illusion because I wanted it to be true and this would solve the mystery?

A few days later, I emailed Matt and told him that he should call me, and I would explain my potential relationship to his family. A week went by without a call or email from Matt, which seemed too suspicious. I wondered: What was going on? Matt finally emailed me back and told me that he would call me that evening. He explained that he has not been on Ancestry.com for a week and just got my email. I didn't know what to believe.

When the phone rang, I felt nervous again. Of course, I told Matt right away the possible connection to his family. I couldn't tell if he was shocked or did not care. I heard no emotion in his voice, nor did he seem surprised.

He told me about his family and his siblings. We chatted for some time. Before our conversation ended, I suggested he do the DNA test. He agreed it would answer the questions of paternity, but he did not say he would take the test.

As I was getting ready to go to bed, my cell phone rang. It was almost 10 p.m. In my family, you don't call before 9 a.m. or after 9 p.m. unless it is an emergency. I saw that it was Mari calling. My first thought was—who calls someone at 10 p.m.? I answered the phone and Mari immediately told me that she wished I had not told Matt.

I wanted to yell and say, "Who calls someone this late?" Instead, I kept calm and said: "I am not going to lie anymore. I am tired of lies in my family, and I am not going to continue this pattern of behavior."

She said she understood but was afraid Matt would tell others in the family. Once more, she emphasized that she didn't want her mother getting hurt.

I told her the truth will always come out in the end. It was not my fault that our parents had an affair. I refused to feel as if it were my fault when I did nothing wrong. Mari told me Matt does not know his niece Lisa knew anything about any of this. Mari wanted to keep it quiet. He doesn't know that Lisa had already sent in a DNA test.

Mari said Matt was ordering an Ancestry.com DNA kit. I told her that was a great idea. However, I wished Mari would also do a test for a closer match, not her daughter, Lisa. I don't understand why Mari did not do the test. Did she have something to hide? But, I was pleased that they had started down this route, since two tests were better than one, and they were paying for their tests. We chatted for a little while, commenting that we will know the answers when the DNA results come back.

Chapter 20: The Calls Keep Coming

Mari called me again later in the week and told me that Matt had told their sibling, Rachael, the whole story. Rachael had called Mari and questioned her until two in the morning. Does this family not sleep? We don't have that in common. I am in bed before 9:30 every night.

Now, three of Billy's children knew about my mother and their father having an affair. Really, four knew. Lisa, the niece, knew, but no one was supposed to know that she knew—except for her mother. I hoped they could keep their lies and stories straight.

Mari informed me that she gave Rachael my telephone number, but she didn't know when Rachael would call. Rachael apparently needed to get the courage to call me. All I could think of was why don't they all wait until the DNA results come in. Then, I thought: I hope Rachael calls at a reasonable time, not after 9 p.m.

A few days later, Rachael called. I believe Rachael to be in her fifties. We started having a very pleasant conversation. Rachael was talking very much like a big sister. She was kind and told me she wished she could be there to hug me. That was sweet of her, I thought. Then, I wondered: Was she drinking? She was very kind to me, a stranger, despite not knowing the DNA results. She was making me feel at ease. So far, she seemed to be the most sensitive family member.

I told her that I did not understand why Billy, knowing that I could be his child, was not reaching out or seeking to talk with me. All the other family seemed to. I got the impression that Rachael had chatted with Billy about the situation. Rachael commented that Billy was scared. I did not probe this statement further, but I repeated that I still did not understand why he hadn't reached out. Our conversation ended with Rachael telling me she would be in town in

April and would like to meet me. I agreed, but I said, "Let's get the DNA results first. We still need concrete evidence."

After I got off the phone, my wife and I talked about my conversation with Rachael. I said that if it were me and I had a possible child out there, I would reach out. I would not ignore this situation. I was having a hard time understanding why Billy did not reach out to me. Yes, I know, we all process things differently. For now, I would wait for the DNA results.

Chapter 21: What Are Your Intentions?

On my way home from lunch, I decided to drop in on Lisa. She owned a small sandwich shop. When I was a kid, I remember the building being a small service station. Since I was in the area, I thought I would meet her for the first time. We had talked on the phone and texted. I thought meeting her in person could break the ice.

When I walked in, she immediately knew who I was. We exchanged pleasantries and talked for about thirty minutes. She was very nice. I was a little nervous at first, thinking this woman could be my niece. We talked about the situation and our families, and we laughed a bit. I showed her a few pictures of my family. We ended our conversation about waiting for the DNA results to confirm any connection. I then headed home.

A few days later, Mari called me, giving me crap for stopping by Lisa's business last week. She asked me what my intentions were. Intentions? Really?

She was accusing me of something I did not understand. She seemed very angry. I told her I stopped in to meet Lisa because I was in the area and wanted to break the ice. I had no intentions, and I did not appreciate her accusing me of having some agenda.

I had been chatting and texting with these people over the last three months. They all have shared family stories with me. What was wrong with my stopping in to meet her? Lisa was a grown adult. Was I not allowed to go innocently and meet her? I was stunned at this accusation, and her asking me what my intentions were.

I think she was angry and taking it out on me. Apparently, her sister, Rachael, had told Jane, another sibling, about me. None of that is my fault. Their family can't seem to keep quiet about any of this. I don't think they can keep secrets. Mari was worried about my intentions. I thought she needed to worry about her siblings blabbing to their mother.

Mari's voice was very cold, making it seem as if I did not matter now. I repeatedly told her that I would not feel bad about any of this. I again explained that I would not lie for her family. Her father and my mother had an affair more than fifty years ago. Whose fault was that?

Her family was afraid it would kill her parents, rip apart their relationship. According to Mari, they have a great relationship. All I could think is, if it's that great, why lie? A relationship based on a lie would not be a foundation I would want to use as the basis for future contacts.

I didn't want to hurt anyone, but none of this was my fault. No one will make me feel ashamed. However, the lies needed to stop. We were all grown adults here.

Mari told me that they would tell the other two siblings who didn't know. I told her that we needed to wait for the DNA results before anyone else knew. Why tell anyone else at this point? The DNA results were not yet available. We couldn't be positive about anything until the results came back.

Our conversation ended, not on the best note. I decided not to answer the phone anymore if Mari called. I wanted to sit back and wait for the DNA results. After all these crazy conversations, I was hoping my DNA was not a match.

My sister Lucy and I were going to lunch and running some errands. When Lucy arrived at my house, I told her about my earlier conversation with Mari and her accusations. She was shocked, just as I was. We both wondered—what do they think my intentions were? All I wanted to know is whether Billy was my biological father. I don't want anything from them except the DNA test.

Did they think I wanted money? Was all this anger based on greed? I didn't get it. They didn't know me at all. I am the least materialistic person you could know. My car was almost twelve years old. I will drive my car for years if it lasts. I couldn't care less about material things. I am not about fashion and the latest trends. I have a simple and great life. All I ask for is the truth.

Chapter 22: Denise's DNA and Other Results

Denise's DNA results finally arrived. Denise was our father's daughter. Now, we knew for sure that our father had one biological daughter.

The next step would be to tell our brother, Greg, the whole story and get his DNA tested. Greg still didn't know about any of this. We didn't want to tell him right away because he lived with our parents. I was afraid he would slip and tell our father about me. I didn't want to hurt our father. Now, the plan was to get Greg alone and tell him the whole truth. First, I needed to order another DNA kit.

I talked with Denise and Lucy about telling Greg the truth. We all had different opinions on the whole situation. We could tell him the genetic test was for genealogy purposes. I felt uneasy about doing that. I decided that I was going to tell him the truth.

The DNA kit arrived by mail within a week. The next step was to go to my parents' house and get Greg alone and tell him the entire story. My wife went with me, and she sat chatting with my parents while I got Greg alone. We only talked for a few minutes, but I told him everything. He agreed to do the test and met me outside so no one would see him doing it.

He didn't seem shocked about anything—not the response I thought I would get. Greg completed the test, and I dropped it in the mailbox on the way home.

Now, all of us were wondering if any of us were a true full sibling. Our situation was a strange thing to wonder. We now knew that Denise belongs to our father. Lucy's biological father was Robert; mine was unknown, and we were waiting to see who Greg's biological father would be.

I was sleeping when Mari tried to call. She left a voice message and a text message. It was late as always when she called, 10:45 p.m. I will say again, who calls someone that late? Is this a habit of hers? Her calling that late was so inappropriate that it made me angry. I saw the text first thing when I woke up in the morning.

She texted me a picture of a computer screenshot of Lisa's DNA results. It showed no DNA match to me. What, no match! I thought, you have got to be kidding. I had concrete evidence that I was not a match to Lisa.

How could this be happening? The family tree we made pointed us to this family. What did we do wrong in constructing our tree? Did Janet and I get this all wrong in our research? Did a connection link me to their family because of my mother's side? We seemed to be so close to an answer. Not having our results pan out seemed weird. We would need to start this process all over again.

Was my mother lying to me and wasting my time? I was trying to take in all this information at 5:00 in the morning—not a good way to start off my morning. I was quite upset. My only thought was—who the hell is my biological father?

Later in the morning, Lisa sent me a text and a picture of her computer screenshot with the DNA results. I guessed that her mother couldn't wait to let me know before Lisa did the same thing. My name was not on her list of matches. She also had texted me a picture of her computer screenshot showing the list of names from Ancestry.com of who she was connected to as first and second cousins. Looking at the picture, I did not recognize any of the names on her list. Lisa texted me that she even called Ancestry.com to double check the results. Since my family tree was private, she wanted to make sure my name would still appear. I had made my tree private after talking with Matt.

Lisa was also surprised by the results. She sent a very nice text back to me hoping I would find the answers and apologized for her family's reactions during the last few months. I thanked her for doing the DNA.

Later that morning, after some searching of the names with whom Lisa shared DNA, I realized all the names seemed to be on her grandmother's side of the family. I wouldn't match to any of them in DNA. Now, I thought, could Mari not be Billy's child, so Lisa's DNA would not match Billy at all? This line of thinking seemed like a bit of a stretch, maybe farfetched, but I still thought there was a chance I could be Billy's daughter. I really needed Billy's DNA.

I did not have enough information to go on. I did not see Lisa's whole list of DNA matches. Did Lisa see any matches in her DNA to her grandfather's side of the family?

Did her grandmother have an affair, and is that why we were not a match? Was Billy not Mari's father? Wouldn't that be a crazy thing? Here Lisa, the granddaughter, does a DNA test for me and did she discover some shocking news about her family? Maybe her mom, Mari, is not Billy's daughter. Wow!

My last chance would be if Matt did his DNA test. Would his results show us as siblings? I guessed now I would have to wait and see if his results showed up on Ancestry.com. There was the possibility of him deleting his results, and I would never know. I hoped that he did the test and was still waiting for his results. I did not want to call him. If his test showed we were not siblings, then I would have to go back to the drawing board. There was no way I would ever get Billy to do a DNA test. My feelings were very conflicted.

In some ways, I was a little relieved that my DNA didn't match. I had a gut feeling when chatting with the potential half-siblings that I probably would not get along with this family. We had too many different values in life.

First, I was a Democrat, and they told me that politics was one thing they didn't discuss. I got the feeling that there were a lot of Republicans in this family. From our discussions, it didn't seem as if there would ever be any discussion on other viewpoints, which was my gut feeling when I looked at some of their Facebook postings. I could tell that we would not agree on many things. Sometimes, you just have that gut feeling and know you will not connect with some people.

However, Lisa could have been my niece, and we got along fine. When I looked at Billy's picture, I still saw myself in him. Maybe that was my mind playing tricks on me because I so desperately wanted to find my biological father.

For now, there was another waiting game. We needed Matt's results to clarify things, or would they? Was Billy his father? Maybe this family had secrets to keep, too. Matt's DNA results never showed up where I could see them on Ancestry.com. Did he even do the test? I will never know.

Chapter 23: The Quest Continues

I decided to order a DNA kit from the company 23andMe. This way I had more chances of getting more and different DNA matches. Maybe others I had not reached could have done a DNA test from 23andMe.

At this point, I needed to do as many DNA tests as I could to find different matches. However, doing these tests was not cheap. The test from each different company can cost about one hundred dollars. Each company shared its results on its own website. Thus, for each company's test, you had to check each different website for your results.

That required me checking each company's website daily to see if I had any new DNA matches. I was determined to do anything I could to get the answers. It seemed the more tests I did, the better my chances were of finding that one important match. It only takes one.

I was running out of ideas to figure out this puzzle. I hoped that the additional test would help Janet and me find the answer. The more tests, the more surnames we had to research to find that one link to provide the answer: Who is my biological father?

Another website on the Internet is called GEDmatch.com. This website helped find the "Golden State Killer" suspect. Here, you can download your raw DNA data from Ancestry.com, 23andMe, or other DNA companies. They take that raw DNA data and provide you with a list of DNA matches from people who also have downloaded their raw data. They give you a list of matches to your DNA so you can compare yourself with others on the site, and they provide the email addresses of the matches so you can contact them directly.

This site seemed to be based on the more scientific side of DNA, with numbers and chromosome segments. I didn't have the patience to fully learn how to understand this site. My friend Janet understood it a lot better than I did and can figure out the math involved. This site allowed us to see others who matched my DNA and who had their DNA tested with other companies.

This site seems to be a central location where people downloaded raw DNA and compared it with others who have done the same. Not everyone uses the same DNA company. GEDmatch.com provides a central location for everyone to download raw DNA data, not just those from Ancestry.com.

As I was processing all this information, I wondered: When I do find my answer, what happens? After all, this has been a secret for more than fifty years. Would I tell my now "play" uncles, aunts, and cousins the truth? Should I tell all my friends who didn't know already? If I do tell my "play" relatives and friends, will my father find out? Maybe I should give people a copy of this book, and they will be able to read the story themselves. I didn't realize until lately how exhausting and emotionally draining it can be to relive the story daily.

Will another family be willing to accept all of this and me? It was a mystery at this point. I send strangers emails trying to get help, and maybe one of them could hold the answers. Or, they could lie— not wanting to confront the truth themselves.

Sometimes while I sit and everything is quiet, I think about all the people who have had shocking DNA results revealed. I belong to a group on Facebook called "DNA Detectives." Every day I read stories similar to mine. People react differently to their situations. As I previously said, I thought of all the family trees that were not correct because of secrets. So many people innocently created their family trees but did not know that their tree was incorrect.

DNA results revealed many affairs. Knowledge of the affairs was changing everything. Much in one's family history can change because of obtaining DNA results. Are people ready for the truth of DNA?

I based my family tree on what my family told me—that my father was my father. Now, what I had learned completely changed my tree. However, as I have previously noted, I will always see the man I have listed as "dad." However, I carry the genes of another man out there.

This week I had sent out many emails to possible cousins who we discovered through each website. I hoped one of them might be able to help. Even though many people ignore their emails, I hoped I would get some answers soon.

I also hope that parents reading this book will be honest with their children about their true heritage. Not knowing is not a good feeling. It has changed the way I see my parents. I realized that they both kept secrets. With Lucy, I wonder what else they are keeping from us.

On the other hand, sometimes I wish I never knew this secret and could go on as I had been. I would keep going on, but now, things were different. I had a hole in my heart that I needed to fill. I wanted to know the answer.

Not getting quick answers about DNA was starting to wear me down emotionally. I spent an enormous amount of time on the computer every day searching. I woke up in the morning, and the first thing I did was turn on my computer, to see if there was any new evidence of who my father could be.

Well, first, I let our dog out and turned on the coffee pot. This search has consumed my time and emotions. Somedays, I needed to stay away from the computer, so I took a break for my mental health.

Chapter 24: Inside a *Seinfeld* Episode with the Costanzas

My mother was still not being helpful. I told her that the DNA results did not match to Billy's family. She didn't seem bothered by this, but kept saying: "It has to be him, I don't get it." Again, my reality was based on Billy's family telling me this. I still did not know 100 percent if they were telling me the truth, which threw me into more confusion.

I thought back on Dr. Gee and what she told me about my biological father, including his last initial. I started to question everything again. Once more, I questioned: Who should I believe?

I don't know why I still tried to protect my mother in all of this and not tell my father the truth and let this secret out. I did not like holding onto this secret. Maybe, if I told him, it would take some stress off me. Was I keeping this secret just because of my mother's health? I still find it hard to keep feeling angry toward my mother. I don't know where I get that trait. Maybe it was from my biological father! I hoped someday to have figured out this trait and much else. My wife told me over and over that it was okay to be angry. However, I have not let myself get to that angry point.

I had another conversation on the telephone with my mother. This time, when I hung up the phone, I felt angry. For the first time, I directly let out my frustration to my mother. Maybe what I needed to do for myself was to let out my anger. I had to realize it was okay, as my wife has said, to feel angry.

Many different emotions were running through my head. The one emotion that made me feel crazy inside was that I couldn't remain angry at my mother because overall, I am a very happy person and I don't let anger control me. When anyone made me angry, I spoke my mind. But, after it was off my chest, I moved on.

My friends knew this about me. I can be angry at one of them, and I will tell them why I was angry; we would talk about it, and then we moved on as friends.

I kept replaying in mind everything that my mother and I have talked about. I questioned things a lot. How could she lie to me my entire life? I have given her many opportunities to tell me the truth. I have flat out asked her—was it a one-night stand, or did something bad happen?

She just said: "I don't remember—it was so long ago."

"You were thirty years old," I said. "I remember stupid stuff I did at thirty." So, I was not buying my mother's story. I still thought she was lying.

With Lucy's secret out, news about my paternity would have been a piece of cake to tell me. Since we were having the discussion, why not tell me the truth? I already knew that the man who raised me was not my biological father. That secret was out. What mother continues to lie to her grown-up child? Was she that selfish that she didn't care?

My sisters and I have talked about her selfishness since finding out Lucy's DNA results. I never really saw or realized that side of my mother. I guess I was seeing it now at fifty years old. She knew Lucy's paternity and kept it from Lucy's biological father all these years. She knew Robert was Lucy's father. What was different with me and my paternity?

I wondered, was this deceitfulness and secretiveness the way my mother was? I always looked at my mother in a different light. Now, it was as if the curtain had come down and the truth was ready to be shown. It was almost like a movie where the ending shocked you. It was rather like writing this book. The more I wrote, the more twists and turns got revealed.

I don't want to believe my mother can live her life full of lies. I don't want to start questioning everything I have done in life. Nevertheless, I started thinking—was I like my mother for being selfish and lying? I hated that thought. I knew I had some characteristics of my mother. She can be caring, sweet, and would do anything to help a person in need. I certainly wanted to keep these positive characteristics. I felt as if my head were about to burst. I needed a vacation. Our vacation could not come soon enough.

As I pulled into my parents' driveway, I noticed a plastic thing in their backyard by the gate. I stared at it for some time wondering, what the hell is that? I started to laugh. My father has always done the strangest things. I could only imagine what this thing in their yard was.

As I mentioned, I often feel as if I were living in a *Seinfeld* episode. Part of this occurs because my father and mother do the craziest things. We call our parents the "Costanzas," George's parents from *Seinfeld*.

I later learned that this mysterious item was a wardrobe bag that my parents had used for shoes. This wardrobe bag now had tomato plants inside. My father repurposed it into a plastic greenhouse with shelves used for plants.

The purpose of my visit to my parents' house was to help my mother get some financial things in order. I realized that lately, she was becoming more confused. I talked to my father about her confusion and the fact that he should take over and learn all the financial paperwork.

When I broached this topic, he seemed to be in denial and did not show any interest in handling the finances. Here I was stuck in the middle of their crisis, and I wanted to scream. I had my stuff to resolve. I couldn't tell him about it, though. It was hard not to blurt out my secret.

I realized my father still has that I-will-ignore-problems, and they-will-go-away attitude. My parents had been married more than sixty years, and my father has never had a credit card or done any of the financial paperwork. He had no idea what was going on financially—what bills they had or about anything that dealt with financial stuff. My mother would give him cash when he asked.

When I tried to talk to him about it, he said, "Your mother takes care of that stuff, I don't." I told him it was time for him to learn. He just ignored that conversation and said he had an appointment. He chose to ignore the fact that my mother was getting worse in her confusion and that he should help out.

I think it was laziness and selfishness on his part. My sisters said, "They are meant for each other." He figured that I would do that stuff, and he did not care. My father's attitude made me want to pull out my hair.

I told my sister Lucy what had happened and how our mom was very confused about everything and our dad just ignored it all. Lucy said that I needed to take over all their financial dealings. I just wished someone else would do this. I had enough on my plate right now. I knew that I was the closest to my mother, and I guessed no one else would feel comfortable doing it. I just wished someone else would step in.

Lucy took over our grandmother's finances when she couldn't do them anymore. I still don't understand why Lucy had to do that and our mother didn't help. Maybe that was another example of our mother's selfishness that Lucy and I had discussed.

It seemed that our mother called us only to remind us of something she needed, but did not call just to say hello anymore. I kept telling myself—it's her health, and I should not take it personally, but doing this was difficult. Anyone with an elderly parent will understand.

It was sad to watch my mother, who once held a powerful position with the military, become so frail and need help. Some days, she did not seem to need help. When I took her to have her taxes completed, she asked the accountant questions that shocked me— detailed questions about deductions and percentages.

I was amazed. I wanted to say: "You can understand all of this, and can't tell me who my biological father is?" Sometimes, I am surprised at what she says and understands. Her changeable behavior made me feel as if I were in a nightmare.

Chapter 25: My Brother Greg's DNA Results

My brother Greg's DNA results arrived. He was not our father's child. Wow! My jaw dropped as I read the results on the computer. All I could say out loud was—"You have to be kidding me." I felt shocked. I was hoping at least one of us had the same father. Now, I have discovered that we all have different fathers. Our family parentage was crazy!

None of us had any full siblings. Within an eight-month period, we went from four siblings growing up to now being four half-siblings. It was crazy to think my mother had four kids by four different men. I thought, this was more than a bit weird—it was embarrassing. If our mother married four times and had four kids by different men, it would have been different. All of us, except for Denise were from her having affairs.

Greg's DNA test showed that he had another half-sister on his biological father's side. Since I administered the DNA test to him, I wondered if this half-sister would contact me through Ancestry.com looking for Greg. She might want answers to her family drama. At this stage, we did not know what further secrets we would learn.

When I told Denise and Jim, her husband, about Greg, both were shocked once again. I was sure her jaw dropped at the results. However, Denise once mentioned to me that one day our father had told her that when he died, we would find out some secrets. We still don't know what he meant by this; Denise did not ask him. I think she was probably shocked that he was saying this to her. Wouldn't he be shocked at what we already knew? What does he have to hide, I wonder?

I still needed to tell Greg the results—that he was not our father's son and that he had another half-sister out there. I had no idea what he would do with this information. I would not keep this secret from him. Now, I needed to figure out—do I tell my mother?

Chapter 26: I Needed a Break

My wife and I planned a little getaway for our fourth-year wedding anniversary. We headed to Pennsylvania to the Nemacolin Woodland Resort. We stayed at Falling Rock—a beautiful place. My wife surprised me and arranged for a butler for us. The butler just happened to be a woman. She was very nice. In the evening, she brought us warm cookies and milk, and lavender salts for the bath. At one point, we asked for an ironing board, and she told us she would iron our clothes.

Of course, we said, "No, you don't have to do that, we will iron our own clothes." We felt like the rich and famous here for a few days. In the morning, the butler delivered fresh juice and coffee to our room. All we had to do was call the butler, and she came right to our room.

While on this trip, we were able to see Kentuck Knob and Fallingwater, houses designed by Frank Lloyd Wright. We were the only ones for a tour of the Kentuck Knob house. Thus, the tour guide gave us our own personal tour. Again, we felt like the rich and famous. All we needed was the butler to bring us cookies and snacks.

The two houses seemed to be ahead of their times in design. Wright built Kentuck Knob in the 1950s and Fallingwater in the 1930s. Kentuck Knob had the coolest chimes outside. The house blended into the woods. Inside this house were original stainless-steel appliances, well before they were popular. Frank Lloyd Wright completed the design for this house at eighty-six years of age, it was the last house he designed.

After Kentuck Knob, we went to see Fallingwater. Fallingwater is a national historic landmark. Many people were visiting this location when we took this tour. A stream ran underneath the house. The views from the house were incredible. I was fascinated by the windows and their designs, which connected to an airflow that kept the house cool without air conditioning. Furniture was built right in place and added charm to each room. This should be a must-see on one's bucket list.

A couple of times while at the resort, we took the shuttle they provided to go to the casino within the resort. My wife has a lucky streak at casinos. She will walk by a machine and say "this machine is lucky, I feel it." Then, she puts a twenty-dollar bill in the machine, hits maximum bet and walks away a winner. When she gets that feeling, she always does well.

I don't have those feelings at the casino. I just play a machine with lots of bells and whistles that look like fun. I wished my wife had the luck to be able to tell me about my paternity. I certainly was not having luck in this either.

While I do not have good luck at picking winning machines, I do get some crazy feelings when I feel a ghost spirit around me. I have had those feelings since I was a child. I have seen and felt many things in my life.

In fact, I had one of these crazy feelings about a ghost on the first night we were at the hotel. I woke up because I heard a woman's voice say to me, "Her name is Lillian." I hoped this name was related to someone I would find in the search for my biological father. Maybe it was my grandmother on that side of the family reaching out? Why in the world would someone say that name to me?

I don't tell too many people about the spirit side that I feel or hear. Some people might think I am a bit crazy. But, I always assure people that, when it happens to them, they will be believers. I told my wife what I had heard that night. She was not too surprised. I tell her about all the things I hear. She hoped that "Lillian" was a clue about who I needed to be looking at for my paternity.

After we left the resort, we headed to "Inn BoonsBoro On the Square" for a night. The author Nora Roberts owns this hotel.

We had reservations in the "Penthouse." This top-floor, beautiful room had a sitting area separate from the bedroom plus a huge bathroom with a tub and separate large shower. It also had a toilet that seemed to do everything on its own, well almost everything. I was amazed at such fancy things.

The afternoon we arrived, we were the only guests. It was an off time and a day after they had a busy weekend. The staff set up a happy hour spread for us with wine and lots of appetizers. I couldn't believe how much food was out, just for us. It was quiet, and the staff was extremely nice.

Since no one else was staying at the inn that night, we were able to see all the different rooms. The innkeeper unlocked all the doors so we could view each room. Each of the rooms in the rest of the inn was different and very charming. Nora had named each for literary lovers. One room was named "Titania and Oberon," in honor the queen and king of the faeries from Shakespeare's *Midsummer Night's Dream*. Another room was called "Nick and Nora," from *The Thin Man* by Dashiell Hammett.

We felt so welcomed. We also enjoyed homemade warm chocolate chip cookies that evening. I even bought my first Nora Roberts' book, *Naked in Death* under her pen name J. D. Robb.

What a beautiful place. The guest services staff were quite nice. We will make a return trip. I only wish we could have stayed longer this time. Next time, we will get a group of friends to go and do some sightseeing in the area. Maybe we will take a local ghost tour, since the Civil War battlefields are nearby.

It was hard for me to leave home for more than a few days at a time because of our dog, Chuck, our angel. Chuck, a standard poodle, was twelve years old. He was registered as a red poodle when I got him at eight weeks old, but he was now beige. When he was a puppy, he had a red color, but at twelve years of age, he was completely beige. Seeing his coloration made me wish I could go from brown hair to darker brown hair, not to gray hair.

People always think Chuck is a golden-doodle, a mixture of poodle and golden retriever. Little kids always say "look at the poodle," but it's the adults who get his breed wrong. I have been cutting his hair myself for his entire life. He lets me do anything to him, cut his hair, clean his teeth. He is like my little son—a sweet dog with a kind soul. He loves older people and kids. We hate to leave him and when we do, we both miss him very much.

When we are away, he stays with my ex-partner, who had known him since he was a puppy, when we brought him home together. Yes, it was weird that my ex-partner kept him, but as the joke goes in the gay community "exes always seem to stay friends." At least, I know when we go away he is doing fine, but we still miss him very much. As he gets older and reaches toward Doggie Heaven, I wondered if we could ever own another dog. He is perfect in our eyes.

Chuck seemed to be my previous dog—was he my prior dog, Willy, reincarnated? He had a look in his eyes that I recognized. I felt as if I have had the same dog for thirty years, which was why Chuck was super special to me. He has been through a lot in life with me. He was there when I met my wife. She fell in love with him, and he loved her right back. Watching the two of them together makes me very happy. I wish she could have seen him as a puppy and have had the whole twelve years I have had with him.

One evening during our vacation, I was watching television when something on the screen sparked a memory for me. I had a "déjà vu" moment. I recalled a dream I had years ago in which I told my ex-girlfriend that my father was not my father. I thought the dream was weird and it made me feel weird. I am not sure why I recalled this dream then, but I called Lucy to tell her. Lucy reminded me that I had told her this dream before.

I guess she remembered me telling her because at the time she had her secret questions about her paternity. Lucy had been questioning her paternity her entire life. It probably did not help that we siblings would tell her how different she looked. However, for her to have remembered this conversation, it must have sparked her memory. I believe things like this happen all the time. We need to open our minds to them. Recalling my old dream about my father not being my father—especially before I discovered that he was not my father—was freaky.

Chapter 27: Back to Reality

Vacation was now over, and my wife had to go back to work. I needed to return to my research to refocus—to figure out what I was missing. Why was it taking so long to figure out who my biological father was?

I almost felt as if I were in the movie *Groundhog Day*, with each day seeming to be a repeat of the day before. Janet and I chatted several times a day about the research and what new things we found. We had many surnames to research. Each new name could lead us in another direction. Certainly, we both wanted to pull our hair out at this point.

Chapter 28: Karen—"Somewhere Over the Rainbow"

Our dear friend Karen passed away from cancer that week. She was the strongest person I have ever known. Her illness never stopped her until now.

The funeral service was at a large Catholic Church filled with friends and family. The church held more people than I had ever seen at a funeral—except at a police funeral. As I sat through the service, I could only think that Karen would be amazed at the turnout of all these people for her. It was a humbling experience to know my dear friend touched so many lives—even with people who I did not know. I can only hope so many of my friends would be there to see me off.

It's funny what you learn about your friends after they are gone. Karen often joked with me about my wife having so many close friends. I never knew Karen had so many friends. I had known her for thirty years, and I was still learning about her.

A few weeks before Karen's passing, she had the opportunity to go to Hawaii for her fiftieth birthday. She flew across the country and enjoyed an amazing time with other friends of ours. Most of her friends, knowing how she was feeling, could not believe she went. She was stronger than any of us could imagine.

We always joked that in another life we would all meet on the beach in Hawaii and be archeologists, because this would be a cool profession to have. Outside, playing on a beach living in Hawaii, getting paid, it all sounded good.

A few weeks after Karen came back from Hawaii, she gave her close friends pink ukuleles. She told us that she wanted each of us to learn the song "Somewhere over the Rainbow." If we were lucky enough ever to see a rainbow, we will know that it was Karen sending us a sign and we should take out our ukuleles and play her song.

The day before Karen passed away, a group of us, her close friends, were at her house having lunch. We were all—including Karen—eating hamburgers and onion rings. I could not imagine that she would pass away the next day. During our visit, we laughed so hard. That is one of the memories I want to retain. Karen said to me on that day: "Hey, guess what? I will know who your biological father is before you."

We both laughed, and I told her, "You better give me a sign of some sort and tell me who he is."

She said, "If you are meant to know, you will find the answers." And that type of generosity and loving soul are part of the reason; I will miss my dear friend every day.

Karen always gave me the best advice for everything. I will miss her advice as well as miss being in her presence. I know all of her friends will miss her every day. She was one of those people who was special to each of us.

A few months ago, I got a tattoo in her honor because of a joke we shared. The tattoo was the cartoon character Fred Flintstone, but with a bit of a twist. He had a fish tail, which reminded me of her last name. While growing up and even as adults, we loved to watch Fred Flintstone. We both collected the Flintstone glass mugs McDonald's gave out. I still had mine. Every day I see this tattoo, I think of my friend.

Karen and I talked and texted everyday like two teenagers. We laughed at the stupidest things. I keep hoping Karen will tell me in my dreams who my biological father is. I know she wants to tell me my answers. Karen could not keep a secret. I am sure if she is an angel or a ghost, she still won't be able to keep a secret. For now, I will have to be patient and wait for the answer, just as she told me.

Recently, I was taking my daily walk when all of a sudden, I heard music. I wasn't sure at first from where it was coming. I then realized it was coming from my phone in my pocket. The strangest thing was that it was playing a song that I had put on a playlist for Karen more than two years ago. How did that happen?

If you have an iPhone, you understand that if you clear off all applications from running, it saves on your battery. I had just done that before my walk, as I do every day. How did my music application open Karen's playlist and play a song from it? I could only wonder, how is this happening? The song playing was by Charlotte Church, "Pie Jesu," from her album, "Voice of an Angel." Was this Karen reaching out to me?

Karen and I talked all the time before her death of how she would come and give me signs of her presence after she died. Was this a sign? I kept wondering about this as a tear ran down my cheek. Was she playing this song? Karen knows I am having a hard time with her death; I lost my best friend.

The day Karen went to hospice, I called my father and told him he would have to take my mother to her doctor's appointment, in a few days. I explained that I did not know what was going to happen to Karen and I needed to be free to go to the hospice location. I could not worry right then about my mother and her appointment in a few days.

My father agreed and said he was capable of taking my mother to her doctor's appointment that week. I should not have been involved in this at all. He should have been the one to take her to the new Parkinson's doctor. He lives with her and will be able to answer questions the doctor might have. My mother, I was sure, would not be happy with me for not going. She doesn't seem ever to want to go anywhere with my father in the car. She would have to understand that I was thinking of my friend Karen, who she knew had been a close friend for years.

As I have grown to expect, my parents had not yet called me in eight days to ask anything about Karen—providing another example of the selfishness that my siblings and I have discussed. They both choose to ignore stuff and act as if nothing happened. One call to check and see what had happened to my friend would have been nice. I questioned their lack of love for any of their kids. If I had kids, I would never want them to feel a lack of love.

Lucy even had a little health scare she shared with our mother the day Karen passed away. Our mother still has never called Lucy to check on how she was doing. She called Lucy that day only because she wanted Lucy, not our father, to drive her to her doctor's appointment that week. Again, they seemed to call us kids only when they needed something, not just to check in and see how we were doing.

I thought back to my childhood and realized that I had never lacked discipline from my parents. I definitely learned to be polite and have manners. But, I never got the push from them urging me to strive toward a goal and accomplish something in life. I don't think my sisters had that either, and my brother was back home living with our parents. I know he never had the push from our parents to succeed in life.

I do, however, remember when I graduated in law enforcement. My father did say that day as he hugged me, "I'm proud of you." That comment will always stick in my head. I think it was the first time in more than twenty years I ever heard those words.

My mother would give me a card that expressed how she felt. It wasn't until I was in my twenties I remember hearing "I love you."

I think that is because I was moving out of state and my mother was sad that I was leaving.

When I was in high school, I cannot recall my parents ever asking to see my report card. I'm sure they must have signed it, but they never commented on my grades. I did not get great grades, and I realized now, I probably had a learning disorder that never was acknowledged. I think the lack of communication with my parents kept me from telling them when I had problems in school. However, my parents never probed or asked about my progress in school or lack of it.

As I was writing this book, a lot of thoughts came to me. For me, secrets are still a very sensitive subject. That is why this whole process touches a deep part of my core. It was hard enough growing up gay and trying to keep that a secret from everyone. So, I understand my mother keeping secrets, at least to a certain point.

When I was a child, I belonged to a Christian youth group. The leader of the group, an adult, frequently would talk about how all gay people were going to Hell. As a child hearing this, I was scared. Was I going to go to Hell? I thought God loved everyone. I could not talk to anyone about it. It was my secret. I didn't choose to be different. I just was. This group confused me more. How could they say gay people were going to Hell? I always thought, did they know stuff I didn't know?

Especially because of the fear of going to Hell and other exclusions of gay people, I was not going to tell anyone I knew that I was gay. Years later, I realized that there were several gay kids in this group. As adults, we all talked about how terrible this "leader" made us feel. I still don't understand why some adults make kids feel bad about who they are. I am glad that the world has become more open. Now, there are different types of identities and relationships, and all people are not straight; and those who are different are no more going to Hell than anyone else. Perhaps, there is a special place in Hell for youth group leaders who put down kids whose identities do not match their own.

I increasingly realized things that stemmed from my childhood. Nevertheless, I am happy that I chose a career on my own and pursued what I wanted. I do regret and wish my parents would have guided their other kids and me more. I don't blame my parents for things. I wish they would have tried harder to understand each of us kids individually.

Chapter 29: More and More DNA Connections

We had received my results from the website 23andMe, so Janet and I had more DNA connections to examine. One DNA connection had a fairly higher percentage of matching than all my previous DNA connections, which could be a good connection and bring us to the answers sooner rather than later.

I have been in contact by email and phone with this third or fourth cousin, Madison through 23andMe. She was trying to help us figure out our connection. My DNA matches with both her and her sister. She has been asking her family questions. I hope she can get us some good clues and bring us closer to an answer.

Madison and her sister, Cate, have been talking to cousins, trying to see if anything matches my situation. So far, nothing has matched. We were able to narrow the search down to their great grandparents' family surname line. I now match DNA through 23andMe and Ancestry.com with six people connected to this family surname. Now, we still can't figure out how I match this surname. Was there a child no one knew about? Perhaps there was a child of an extramarital affair? Lots of things could make this connection hard to find, but we will keep looking.

Chapter 30: My Friends' Stories of Adoption and Birth Parents

As I talked to my friends, I realized many of them had stories—some similar to mine but others very different. We all went through crazy life situations. How each of us handled these situations was what made us unique individuals.

Sidney's Story

My friend Sidney was born in 1966. Here is her story:

I've known I was adopted for as long as I can remember. My adoptive parents, Phil and Carol, would read me a children's book that told the story about how I came into their lives. The book they read wasn't really about me, but the adoption agency must have had books made for different situations that could be used by the new parents.

My mother was in her late thirties and my father forty-one when they brought me home. They had two boys, a biological son named Phil, after my father and grandfather, and an adopted brother, Gary. Phil was eleven years older than I was and Gary was four years older. My parents always wanted more children, but my mother had a skin infection after giving birth to Phil, and she believed that the antibiotic she received made her unable to have more children. No one has proved whether her belief was true, but my parents looked at it as it a sign from God that they were to be given two children that they didn't conceive.

My parents were devout Catholics and raised us the same. All of us children went to the same Catholic grade school from first through eighth grade. Then, the boys went on to a private boys high school, and I went to a private girls high school.

I had what a lot of people would consider a fairy-book childhood. I grew up in a row house of mainly young working-class families. I walked to school every day. My mother was a stay-at-home mother and participated in my school activities.

I had lots of friends of all ages and both sexes. I was a little tomboy and loved sports and getting dirty. Our neighbors would come together to play games, go sleigh riding in the winters, and participate in open houses during the holidays so that neighbors could see each other's decorations and exchange gifts. My parents took us on annual summer vacations to the beach. We would celebrate milestones with the extended family whenever possible.

I never had anything truly tragic happen in my life as a child. But, I always felt a hole in my heart. Not knowing where I came from and who I looked like weighed on me. I remember coming downstairs on Christmas morning, and everyone was in the basement ready to open gifts. I would stop at the manger in the living room and get on my knees and pray to God to help my biological family get through the day because I knew they were sad without me. I felt the same sadness on my birthday. I always wondered how my biological parents felt on the day I was born.

I couldn't tell Phil and Carol about this because I knew they wouldn't understand. On various occasions, I asked them if they had any information about my biological family. They would say they didn't. But, one thing they would eagerly share was that my origin was Irish and German, just like theirs.

When I graduated from college, my parents gave me all the documentation they had from the adoption agency. It was information that was more pertinent to their experience when I was handed over to them. I found out around this same time that I had been in foster care for the first thirty days of my life, but as a child, they would say that they got me right away. I knew from baby pictures that this wasn't true. I didn't look like a newborn in the earliest photos.

When the Internet first started, I found some websites for adoptees that had databases that you could join to see if you could find a match to a parent. I paid for a few of the more major sites but was not successful in matching with anyone.

One day, I went to have my hair cut, and my stylist told me that she had just lost her father. I told her how sorry I was and she proceeded to tell me that there was a silver lining to his death. She had found her biological father and was ecstatic.

The state had recently changed the law to allow adoptees to find their parents, as long as the consent was mutual. I immediately went home and contacted the adoption agency listed on the paperwork that Phil and Carol had given me years prior.

The adoption agency sent me a bundle of forms that needed to be witnessed and notarized. I also had to write a letter about why I wanted to find my parents. I had numerous reasons. When I was in my early twenties, I had a medical issue that concerned me, and I wanted to know what my family history was for diseases and other physical problems. At that time, my adoptive parents said they would hire an attorney to see if we could have my records opened so I could know if I had something about which I should be concerned.

Even though they said this, their faces and hearts said something different. I could tell this was not something they wanted me to do. So, I let it go. I found it strange that they were so insecure about me knowing about my biological parents. Now, looking back, I don't think I would have been mature enough in my early twenties to deal with what I would come to learn.

My other reason for pursuing my biological family was that I had never known what it was like to look like someone else. I always found it fascinating to see my friends and their family's similarities. I selfishly wanted to know what that feeling would be.

Being interviewed by one of the social workers from the adoption agency was the last step in the process. I went to the office of the adoption agency, and the social worker asked me all sorts of questions; she wanted to make sure I was mentally stable and that I was, indeed, Sidney.

When we finished, she said that it could take weeks, even months, to find a match and that she would be in touch when she knew more. I left her office and drove straight home, which took about fifteen minutes. As I walked in the house, my home phone was ringing. It was the social worker saying she believed she had found my biological mother. Apparently, because of my biological mother's circumstances, not much had changed with her personal information since I was given up for adoption, so it was easy for them to locate her.

The social worker began to tell me a little about her. At this point, she did not give me any names—just non-identifying information. First, she said to me, "If you need counseling, we can get you someone who specializes in this sort of thing." Now, looking back on that, I would guess that my family situation was somewhat unique.

I thanked her and sat at the kitchen bar and just listened in amazement. My mother, now known to me as Becky, was fifteen when she became pregnant with me. She had lived in a home with parents who married and divorced each other twice. At the time, she got pregnant with me, her mother had remarried a local businessperson. Becky, her biological brother, and half-sister lived in a dysfunctional home. Her mother, Minnie, was a local real estate broker.

Minnie told Becky that she would either raise me as her sister or she would have to give me up. Becky hated her life in that home and didn't want her mother raising me. My biological father had just graduated from the same high school Becky was attending, and he had already moved to another state with his parents after graduation. Her parents sent Becky to a home where pregnant unwed girls went to wait to have their babies.

While Becky was away, her parents moved to another area of the county so that neighbors wouldn't know that they had sent Becky away. By the time she had me and signed the paperwork, my biological father, Donnie, had shown up to be with her. It was too late to change the situation; the legal documents were processed, and I was already with my foster family. Donnie stayed with Becky and they married. They moved to Virginia so that Donnie could join the Coast Guard and get job training.

Becky became pregnant again almost right away with my brother, Chip. We are sixteen months apart. They later had another boy, Dean. Becky and Donnie were married for thirty-one years when Donnie was killed by a drunk driver while riding his motorcycle to a friend's house.

It was no wonder the social worker was concerned about my mental state after I learned some of the particulars about my biological family. She asked me how I would like the introduction to happen between Becky and me. I told her that I wanted to be the one to contact her.

The first time we spoke, Becky was very emotional on the phone and extremely impatient about wanting to meet me. We set up the day and time and met at their family home. I took my partner, now wife, to this encounter on a spring afternoon. I remember getting out of the car and Becky's friend pointing at me and saying, "that is your daughter," because she thought Becky would be mistaken as to which one of us was Sidney.

We hugged, and Becky looked at me and said, "What's it like to look at yourself?" I was overwhelmed, almost speechless, which isn't normal for me. For the first time I think ever, I didn't know what I was feeling. It was like it wasn't real.

When I was very young, I would have a recurring dream. My adoptive parents would take me to New York City every year to see Broadway shows and have meals at fancy restaurants. I loved it there. But, for some strange reason, I would have this dream where I would go into a public restroom with my mother and we each would go into our own stall. When I would come out, this person, who looked just like my mother, would take me and throw me over the Brooklyn Bridge. I would wake up every time I felt my body falling. I had this dream until I was a young teenager.

It was rather funny to me how small Becky was. Even though there were similarities about our faces, she was about 5 foot nothing, and I am close to 5 feet 8 inches. I have a sturdy build, and she had a small frame. We went on her back deck and drank iced tea and started discovering things about each other. I asked about our family genealogy, and she said that I was mostly English. My adoptive mother and father wanted to believe that I was of the same descent as they were. I don't know why they thought that was important. It made me a bit angry when I learned differently. Becky also told me my name on my birth certificate.

We also discovered that the reason we didn't have a match on the adoptive websites was that Becky had my birthday off by a number. She confused the day I was born with my biological father's birthday. Becky had also gone to the State Assembly and fought to get the law passed to allow birth parents and legal-aged children to give mutual consent so they could learn the identity of each other. Becky said she always was looking for me. She told me that Donnie couldn't talk about me; it upset him too much.

For the most part, it was a very exciting and enjoyable day for us both. Even though I was not looking for a "Mother" because I already had one, it was nice finally to put a face to my birth mother. The part that overwhelmed me was walking through their home and seeing all these familiar faces in pictures of people I had never met before. It was surreal.

What I found out that day was that my brother, Chip lived with her; she had only that day informed him of my existence. He had to call an aunt to confirm what Becky had told him about having a sister. To say he was upset was an understatement. Chip had lots of baggage, just like his mother.

The family had lost their father/husband tragically, and the younger son, Dean, had died in his late twenties. Dean suffered from drug and alcohol addiction most of his adolescent years. He was in and out of military school and rehabilitation centers into his twenties. At the last place he was drying out in Colorado, he met his wife and mother to his son who also had addiction issues.

They had a civil marriage and came back to where both of their families lived so they could start their family together. Dean's wife, Mary, was raised Catholic and she wanted their marriage to be recognized in the Catholic Church. So, they attended the mandatory classes run by one of the priests in her parish. At the last class, the priest informed them that he didn't think that Dean was ready to be married. Dean quibbled, that they were already married and he was trying to do the right thing for his family. Becky always said that this was what brought Dean back to his dark place, and he ended up hanging himself in the family basement. His wife had their child, Jimmy, soon after Dean's death. Jimmy was currently in his last year of military high school where his mother's fiance' lived.

Chip and Becky worked for the family's court reporting business while Donnie was alive. The funny thing is that Donnie taught a few classes at a college where my parents wanted me to go to learn how to be a secretary. My birth father was a court reporter.

However, being a secretary was not something I wanted to do. I didn't want to serve coffee and get other people's dry cleaning when I was that age.

Chip handled the day-to-day operations of the business, and Becky was the person who collected payment from clients and paid the bills. She said that she was the only one who was tough enough to get it done. Donnie and Chip wanted everyone to like them, so they didn't want to get their hands dirty, which was funny because I'm the bad cop in our business—managing vacation rentals.

Becky had to leave the business in her late thirties because doctors diagnosed her with Multiple Sclerosis (MS). The MS was giving her mobility issues and blurred/double vision.

After the day Becky and I met at her family home, she told me that Chip would be in touch with me after he had time to process the news. When Chip was in high school, he got his girlfriend pregnant. He thought he would marry this girl, but they knew they weren't equipped to do so at such a young age. So, the families got together and decided to put the baby up for adoption. All these years had passed, and neither Donnie nor Becky had ever told him about me. The perfect opportunity would have been when Chip discovered his girlfriend was pregnant. Chip was so angry that they never told him, and he went through all that pain of thinking that they didn't understand him.

Chip called me. We now have had a friendship for many years. But, there was always a feeling as though he wanted a wedge between Becky and me because he didn't have a healthy relationship with her. Upon Becky's passing from complications of MS, Chip and I had a falling out that I believe is irreconcilable.

Becky and I had many years of off-and-on communication. I was living on the other side of the country. Most of the time we knew each other, the dysfunction between Chip and Becky was

138

draining on me. On top of this, Becky would be dating men who Chip hated. I was put in the middle to play referee most of the time. Being in this situation kept me from ever getting close to them as an immediate family member would do.

I have had days over the years that I was grateful to have found my biological family and connected all of the dots. And, I've had days when I wish I hadn't. Life is complicated. Helping two families to get along can be quite draining. However, it has fulfilled that feeling of knowing where or to whom I belong.

Sidney

Lynn's Story

My Uncle Saul was a doctor in the early 1960s. He was the type of doctor who went from house to house in addition to his practice. He carried a black medicine bag and treated all types of people, regardless of their background.

My birth mother was seeing him for prenatal care. She told him she wasn't going to be able to raise me since she was very poor and her previous three children had been taken from her by the state for neglect.

My uncle, knowing that my adoptive parents were trying to conceive but had not been successful, arranged for my adoptive parents to adopt me from birth. I was taken from my birth mother immediately after I was born and placed in the arms of my adoptive parents.

I have always known I was adopted. My parents told me as soon as I could communicate that I was their "chosen" child. They eventually had two biological children, my brother and sister. My adoptive parents made me feel special—I was the one they chose. They were transparent about my history and told me everything they knew about my adoptive mother. The funny thing is that I always thought they were holding back, but I found out later that everything they had ever told me was true. I think transparency is the best way to deal with adoption.

I grew up in an entirely Jewish community but had blonde hair as a child with blue eyes. I looked distinctly different than my adoptive family and my community. I also felt different. I had a different, more intense disposition than my adoptive family.

I remember sitting at the dinner table one night and examining my brother's and sister's features and then looking at my parents to see the origin of those features. I wondered what it was like to have that experience, to look like your family.

In the 1990s, I was made aware of a state law that enabled me to see a redacted copy of my birth certificate. The law allowed for a caseworker to be assigned to my case and to begin trying to find my birth family. The law permitted, if the birth parents were open to it, to connect birth parents with the child given up for adoption.

The social worker had a very difficult time finding my birth mother. She found out pretty quickly that my birth father was deceased. My birth mother was living in a home in Indiana, and the theory was that she was mentally ill. I had five or six siblings. The social worker said they were all drug addicts, alcoholics, or in jail.

My mother's sister yelled at the social worker on the phone and said, "What the hell does she want? She's the only one that made it!" I considered those words carefully and decided she was right. What did I want? I was suddenly SO grateful that I was adopted out.

My longing to meet my birth mother was fading. My social worker said she would not even see her other children. I felt as if this chapter were closing, although I would have liked to have had a picture. I am at peace with it.

The social worker was amazing. She finally sent me my redacted birth certificate; however, she left it clear enough for me to see everything. Now, I have the information I've always wanted!

I searched for my birth father's obituary and found it easily online. Usually, the obituaries tell about the family and list names that provide good information. So, I saw that he had four brothers and one sister. I focused on the sister, Vicky. I found her address easily online. I sent her a picture and a letter saying I was wondering if I could have some information on her brother, who I believed to be my birth father.

A package arrived at my home in a few weeks. I opened the package, and suddenly I was staring at a picture of a man who looked just like me. I held the picture with my mouth open, simply stunned that this moment had arrived. She had included three pictures and a lovely letter. I called her to speak with her, as her letter invited me to do.

I was quite nervous. I paced the floor while we were talking. I learned that my birth father's favorite song was Sinatra's "I Did It My Way." That was so much like me, I thought! He was 100 percent Italian. He was a ladies' man and brought a new woman to dinner every time he came over. His sister described him to me and said he was always her favorite brother. She was delighted to connect with me.

Vicky was quite gracious. She invited me to come to Maine to meet her and her husband. I was extremely nervous, but I made the trip. I looked like her; we have the same eye color and skin tone. She said she saw the resemblance. The other brother, who was still alive, stopped by and said I had his nose. I had always wanted to get a nose job, but suddenly, my Italian nose was beautiful. We ate salami and drank cheap Chianti and enjoyed our visit. I left with an understanding of where I came from, and I was so very grateful for Vicky and her husband.

We kept in touch until she and her husband passed. I can't describe to someone who isn't adopted how it feels to look and feel so different from your family of origin. No matter how loving they are, no matter how privileged they are, you will always have on your psyche the indentation of being adopted.

Being adopted was the best possible outcome for me, and I'm forever grateful to my parents and Uncle Saul. I could easily be an addict, dead, or in jail. I've had a great life, and I adore my adoptive brother and sister. My adoptive father is still alive, and he is a good man. I feel blessed.

Lynn

Todd's Story

I've always believed everything happens for a reason—whether good or bad, either expected or unexpected—this one thing can change your course of life. If you asked me what my life has been like up to the beginning of this year, I would say pretty incredible. If I were ever given the option to start my life over from the day I was born, I would say "no" a million times over. Since I'm forty-six years old and you probably don't want to read about my entire life, I'll highlight some of the incredible things that have transpired in the first three months of 2017.

My name is Todd. I was adopted at birth in northern California by the best parents anyone could have. Growing up, I always knew I was adopted. I knew what it meant to be adopted, but I never felt different or uneasy about it. Sometimes, I would wonder where I came from, the situation that resulted in me being put up for adoption, and who my biological parents were.

My parents didn't know much about my biological parents. When I would ask, my mom would tell me that my mother had blonde hair, blue eyes, and was artistic. I never felt the need to look for my biological parents, but now and then, I would fantasize about them.

Since I didn't know who they were, I reasoned that they could be anybody. My parents could be movie stars who gave me up to have a career or an athlete who just got someone pregnant. In reality, I already had a loving family with two parents, two sisters, grandparents, aunts, uncles, and cousins. If you didn't know I was adopted, you would never be able to guess.

The idea of figuring out who my parents were would pop up now and then. There were certain ways to try and locate them, but, who knew if it was worth it. I have a cousin who was also adopted. She found her biological family, and it turned out to be a disaster. Sometimes, out of curiosity, I would research different ways to try and locate my biological parents. I really couldn't tell you why I would do that, but sometimes, I just would (there must be a reason).

I looked into hiring a private detective but then thought it wasn't worth the money and who knows if who they found would be my parents. I looked into websites that had open forums where you could put up information on yourself in hopes that one of your biological parents was looking for you.

I even started researching California laws on adoption. Amazingly, California has some really good adoption connection programs run by the state, which fits into more of my story later.

So, even with all of these options, I never felt the drive to follow through with any of my options. As I've grown older, gotten married, and have had children of my own, I started to realize that there was a problem with being adopted. Sometimes it would seem like a very small issue and other times it would seem like a big deal.

This problem started to wear on me, but I would shrug it off because I didn't have any options to fix it. Or did I?

My main problem with being adopted was that I did not have any FAMILY MEDICAL HISTORY! Every time I went to see a doctor, the doctor would ask, do you have any heart disease, cancer, or any other medical issues in your family's history? My answer would always be, "I don't know. I was adopted."

I'm pretty healthy, but just the thought that I could have some medical issue or that I should be doing some preventative maintenance started to bother me.

In December 2016, after a year and a half of sadness and stress (I lost my mom to heart disease in July 2015 and one of my sisters to suicide in December of 2015), I was sharing stories with the author of the book you are currently reading. She was telling me about everything that was happening with her family because of a DNA test through Ancestry.com.

During our conversation, I told her my wife was looking into Ancestry.com and was talking about sending for the kit to see if I could find my biological parents. At that moment, I was talked into it. "I'll help you," the author said. "There are so many tools....you never know; your parents might be looking for you."

I went home and told my wife about our conversation. The next day she ordered two DNA tests so we both could test. When the test arrived a few days later, I figured it would be best to get it done. So, I spit in the test tube, filled out the forms, and mailed it off about a week before Christmas. I never expected what happened next; but, everything happens for a reason!

On December 27, 2016, my wife received an email from a woman who said, "I'm searching for my adopted son who was born in Los Angeles, January 5, 1971." Was this a joke? How did this woman find me and why was she contacting me now? Was this some scam? My wife thought about it, and after reading the email again, we realized it was from an adoption message board she had posted on almost six years ago.

One of the times we were starting to search for answers, we found a website called Adopted.com. My wife put up a small post saying "born in March 1971 in California." We never received any other messages since it had been put up. Why now?

My first reaction was—this is a fluke, it's not my biological mom. I also felt a little protective and unsure of how much information I should send to this stranger. So, I sent a return email saying, "Hello, I'm sorry I don't think we are a match. I was born on March 4, in Northern California. Thanks for reaching out and good luck with your search."

As I already mentioned, I decided to try the matching available on Ancestry.com.

The next day I get another message from this same woman questioning how I knew where I was born. I told her that it was because of my birth certificate. That got me thinking. I started doing some more research. I found that birth certificates are usually amended or changed with adoptions, so there was a possibility that I was her son (but, I didn't think so at that moment. I needed to do more research).

We learned that both her son's adoption and mine were through Catholic Charities, an organization involved with a lot of adoptions in the 1940s-1970s. It was very common for this agency to move the children around from city to city, change birth dates (even as far as forty days from their real birth date), and much more.

I had this woman's name, so I looked her up on Facebook. I found her quickly and realized I had her eyes! Could this be my mom? Gaining this option was too good to be true!

We connected on Facebook, and she shared her story. I learned everything about her. She had just completed a DNA test with 23andMe and was also waiting for the results. She told me that she became pregnant and gave birth in Los Angeles when she was sixteen years old.

The more she told me, the more this was turning into a fairy tale. I'd love to tell the whole story, but this is someone else's book—not mine. I learned so much about her family and life that I joked around that if I wasn't her son, she could pretend I was.

Every day, I would go back and forth. Was this my mom or am I just helping her by talking to her and possibly easing her pain of giving up her son for adoption? Giving up her son for adoption was something she had always regretted. Things would connect us; we would think we were a match one minute, but, then, we would find something that would tell us we weren't. We couldn't wait to get our DNA results back.

In January, we both received our DNA results back from the respective companies. Neither of our families could figure them out since the information from each of the companies couldn't cross over. We found other issues when we tried to research the family trees I had available to me on Ancestry.com.

It turned out that her mother was also adopted (which her daughter didn't even know), so that left us with a dead-end not knowing any true family history or surnames to research on her side.

At that point, we both decided to access the other's DNA test sites. I took the DNA 23andMe test, and she took the Ancestry.com test. We kept in touch and had become very close. I would check the sites multiple times a day hoping to see our answer.

After waiting five agonizing weeks, I was the first to get my results. We were not a match. I wasn't surprised. Deep down, I knew we weren't; I just wanted it to be a great story. Our personalities were too different. However, the hoped-for connection makes a great story.

So, now, that I knew I wasn't related to the woman who contacted me and I could be anyone's son, I started reaching out to the matches I had on both Ancestry.com and 23andMe. On both sites, I had two second cousins with whom I matched.

I thought this would be easy. As long as someone responded to emails, I'd be able to find at least one of my biological parents.

The first contact was on Ancestry.com, and she hadn't logged on since the summer before. Even though I messaged her several times, she never responded. The second cousin with whom I matched on 23andMe responded right away! Only, she told me that she, too, was adopted. After learning her story and getting to know her, we found that we were a match on my mother's side.

So, with the few clues I had, I was determined to either find her mom or mine. My thinking was that if I find one, they surely will tell me who the other is since they would be cousins. Again, this part of the search involved another amazing story, and I'm doing my best to make it a happy ending for everyone with my search.

Now, I'll move on to the crazy part of my story. I had two fourth cousins from Ancestry.com who gave me some surnames to help in the search. One of them helped build a family tree on his side of the family to help me. From 23andMe, I had a strange fourth cousin who would never answer any of my questions directly. So, I had to interact with her in a way so that I could get my answers from what she did not tell me.

I guess "strange" would be the best way to describe her because she was very helpful and instrumental in what happened. After about a week, we had a pretty good family tree built from my Ancestry.com cousin. I took some surnames and sent them to the cousin from 23andMe.

I made my message simple; I asked: "Do any of these surnames look familiar?" Her response seemed a little weird to me. She asked how I got a certain name on my family tree. In my head I thought—because we are related, that's how!

She then told me that she had hired several ladies who specialized in genealogy to help build her family tree, but when they got to this particular person, they couldn't figure out who he was married to or if he had kids. She wanted to know more, and would only tell me that this was her great-great-grandfather.

Being the person who I am, I still wanted to help. I told her I would get what information I could off the tree and send it to her. At first, I didn't realize it, but, this was my connection.

If she were related to a person on my fourth cousin's tree, then that's where I should be looking.

I was not even thinking about the connection. I just started looking at the details of the person on whom she needed information. I wrote down his wife's name, then their children's names. That's when it hit me!

One of the sons was married to a woman whose maiden name matched the other fourth cousin from Ancestry.com. I then realized: this was my connection, and I must be from this line. It wasn't hard from there. This couple had two boys, and I realized that one of them was my biological father! I did some research based on obituaries and newspaper articles and found that they were in the area where I was born around the time I was born. Because of the age, I figured my father was the younger brother, so I tracked him down. After several emails, messages, and even talking to his wife (I didn't tell her anything other than I was doing some research on Ancestry.com), I got to talk to him. It turns out, it wasn't him, but he figured it was his brother. The next day, his older brother contacted me.

To sum up an amazing story without going into all the details I'll leave you with this. Yes, I found my biological dad. He never knew about me. We don't know who my biological mom is. We thought we did, but it wasn't her. My biological father lives down the street from my best friend. He did a DNA test through 23andMe, and we matched DNA—he is my father.

My biological grandmother was still alive. Her maiden name connected all of this. I now talk to all of them on a regular basis. The story is ongoing and great. A few months after I found my biological father, I started searching again for my biological mother. Everything happens for a reason and when it's my time to find her, I will.

Todd

My Thoughts on Secrecy

Todd's story brings me to my thoughts about adoptees. Is it fair to an adoptee not to know who his or her birth parents are? I think it's only human to want to know. I think adults should have the right to know from where they came. Not knowing who your parents are causes a hole of uncertainty that I and others in this position want to fill. That is my choice. But, there is the possibility of disappointment in the answers we may find. I believe we all should have the right and the choice to find the answers about our biological identity—whatever the outcome. Richard Hill, the author of the foreword of this book and the memoir *Finding Family: My Search for Roots and the Secrets in My DNA* (2012) wrote:

"Growing up with an unknown ethnic background is something that bothers many adoptees. In my case, I grew up not even knowing about my adoption."

I also grew up not as adopted but not knowing the entire truth. I now understand feeling left out and in the dark. I feel as if I have an empty space. So, I might understand how some adoptees feel.

Richard Hill wrote his mother a letter about being adopted—a topic that his family avoided for thirty-five years. This lack of communication brings me to my thoughts of wishing my mother would have told me that the father who raised me was not my biological father. Why keep that secret and have me find out only when I was fifty years old? Was I not ready to know the truth? Did she hope that I would never discover this?

Reading Richard's book, *Finding Family*, I also see a communication gap that happened in his family. His mother did not tell him he was adopted because she did not want her son to be discriminated against back in the 1940s—something that commonly occurred among adoptees. He explains in his book:

I was beginning to grasp the different thinking that prevailed in the 1940s'. Now I could guess why I had gone all through elementary and high school without ever encountering an openly adopted child. Their families were also sidestepping prejudice by not talking about it.

It seems many parents in those generations did not want to discuss personal issues. Even when I attended school in the 1970s throughout the 1980s, adoption still was not discussed. If it did come out, it was something you kept quiet. Nowadays, people do talk about adoption, and it is no longer a subject that is kept quiet or seen as shameful.

Other friends of ours have had children by going through an agency and getting artificial insemination. Through discussions among the mothers of a group of their school-age children, they learned that several of the kids in the same school our friend's kid attend were related. Their parents all had artificial insemination. Apparently, several of the couples used the same sperm donor. They did not know, of course, until their kids met and the mothers talked with each other.

I was shocked when I heard this story. I could only think— what if those kids dated and got married. Their children might have had major genetic problems, which is why there are laws against close relatives marrying.

I have my own opinions on how all of this should be regulated. First, I think a onetime "donation" of sperm is all one person should get paid to do. I think multiple donations to a diverse group can cause problems. I don't know much about state-to-state regulations, but it would seem a database is needed to help keep track of donors, and a onetime donation is enough. Otherwise, kids in another state may all end up with the same sperm donor, and when they began dating, they might unknowingly face the consanguinity problem. That makes no sense to me, and I question that whole process.

Chapter 31: "Don't Forget to Enjoy the Journey"—The Next Chapter in My Life

As I process my story, I don't know what to expect. I still feel blank. A million different thoughts run through my head every day. Then, when I reflect on how my friend Karen went through all the horrible aspects of cancer and how rough this process of cancer treatment was on her, it puts my life in true perspective. Despite all the uncertainties I now feel, I am thankful to be alive and have the love of friends and relatives—including "play" relatives. I only hope that I will get some answers.

As Janet and I continued to look at DNA matches, we started building mirrored trees, which allows you to take the family tree from someone who matched your DNA, and you copy their tree. Then, you take another DNA match and copy their family's tree. You keep doing this with the goal of finding a common ancestor to tie all of the trees together to show how you all connect with your DNA. In doing this, you are building a large tree. As this big pool of names grows, you are looking for that common meeting place to see how you connect—to discover who is the common ancestor—that allows two or more people to connect their DNA. One shared ancestor can help guide you in understanding how your DNA matches to others. Doing so is like trying to get from point A to B and meeting at a common ground, which works well with Ancestry.com, since people have family trees in this database.

We also have taken DNA-matched names from other sites looking for a common ancestor match. Increasingly, I realized how challenging family trees could be.

Finding births out of wedlock, adoptions, and name changes throws a lot of things off balance. All of these occurrences increases the difficulty of searching. When we have these issues, we need to be resourceful and come up with other ways to try to discover what we want. Sometimes, searching through newspapers and obituaries helps. References to someone in these documents may help us understand how that person connects.

I wish there were easier ways for genealogy DNA sites to combine trees and follow DNA with a click of a button. My stress level would be greatly reduced if there were an easy way to follow my DNA results and that of others. Having an easier path for searching would make hunting for an unknown parent much more laidback.

My friend Janet, her sister, and her brother, all ordered DNA kits from Ancestry.com. Maybe soon they also will know the truthful answers to questions they have in their own family. Remember, I said earlier we thought "it was in the water." Maybe Janet and I are related. That would make both of us laugh.

For now, I need to figure out how to get rid of the distant feelings I have about my parents. These are emotions that I never imagined I would feel. On some days since making these discoveries, I wish I never knew any of these secrets. Nevertheless, with all that has happened in my life and the stress I have been under during the last year, I will always remember what my dear friend Karen would say to me: "Don't forget to enjoy the journey. Life does go on. We choose how to live it."

We will continue working and searching. Maybe, we will get lucky, and I will check the computer, and a great match will appear in my DNA results. That will end this whole search and start another chapter.

As I previously mentioned, I read John Bradshaw's book *Family Secrets: The Path from Shame to Healing* (1995, Bantam Books). Unfortunately, he is now deceased, but his books are useful to help people understand themselves and their families. I wonder if getting the answer about who my biological father is will be a disappointment to me. What if my biological father is someone I will regret to have found? How will I feel then?

Of course, I don't know what will happen, and I can't control life, but I need to understand as much as I can. Then, I can shut this chapter of the unknown in my own life and move forward and accept what happens, good or bad.

Bradshaw reminds us: "The tough part is that you, like all the rest of us, must learn that no one has any magical powers to save us. Our parents are only men and women, not witches and wizards." Whoever my biological father is, he can't save me from the secrets and lies my mother has told. But, I hope my discovery will give me some closure about the unknown.

My optimism enables me to understand the anger I have felt about the lies and secrets my parents have kept. I wonder if my mother will ever heal her guilt. I could not stand to carry the guilt she must have. Or does she not have guilt anymore? Does she feel uneasy around all her kids now that we all know the truth? I know all my siblings must share some of the same disappointment that I feel about our mother. It makes me feel sorry for our mother.

Laurie and I like to go to the casino now and then and take our chances. It gives us both a break and we have fun. We take a set amount of money, and when it's gone, we leave. We also leave if we win a lot of money. Yes, we could stay and spend our winnings, but we walk away happy. On a recent Saturday afternoon, we had lunch at our favorite local pub and headed to the casino. We were almost at our spending limit when I decided to sit down at my favorite quarter slot machine. Laurie came and sat next to me to play another machine. As I pushed the bet max button, I thought to myself: Karen, if you are here and with me, let me get the three triple stars and win. At that moment, the stars appeared. I got the three triple stars at the maximum quarter bet. As always, I had no idea what I had won. Laurie had to tell me. I said to her, "Did I win a couple of hundred dollars?"

"No, you won a lot, try two thousand dollars. You bet the maximum," Laurie told me.

As we smiled, I told her what I had said to Karen before pushing the button. Now, again, I truly believe that Karen was with me. "Thanks for the cash, Karen. And the next time I see a rainbow, I hope it will have my father's name at the end of it."

Chapter 32: The End Is Never Clear

A year and half has gone by with me only having third- to distant-cousin DNA matches. Some days it is disappointing, and I must walk away from the computer. When I finally got two third-cousin DNA matches to work with, one match wouldn't respond to any emails. The other finally responded but was of little help, and then she would not answer any more emails. I never heard back from her again. Seems a lot of people don't care to help. This is all disappointing. Janet and I knew exactly where each of these DNA matches fits in the working tree. After a year and a half of mapping my DNA matches, we could figure how others seem to tie together, but we just didn't have the answer to where I fit in the big picture.

I would have liked it if we had more details on family links we were stuck on. Of course, I would have liked it if people had responded to the emails Janet and I both had sent to many people. Just a pleasant response to acknowledge the email would be the polite thing to do. Can you help or not, is all we have asked for. I realize people can be rude or show they don't have compassion or manners.

Some matching links we had not figured out, but we kept trying. Since the last census record was recorded in 1940, any records after that year we looked to the Internet for obituaries, newspapers, and any clue we could find to fill in the tree further down the surname lines of these unknown families. Janet and I continued to work a little every day, waiting for that one clue.

Finally, we got a big clue on Ancestry.com and a better clue when this DNA match put his DNA on the website GEDmatch.com: a young man who matches me with the X chromosome. This could be a big break. Now we could start searching his mother's side. We already knew he matches me on my biological father's side. He is a higher fourth-cousin match with the X chromosome. Everyday Janet and I expanded the tree trying to find how I connect to this cousin.

We have exchanged many emails, and he wanted to help. How does he connect DNA to the others we both link? Now we needed to figure how he fits into an already large working tree. At this point we had 47,333 names in the working tree mapping all my highest DNA matches. We were looking for that one common ancestor to give us the answers to link all of this. It seems after Ancestry.com puts their DNA kits on sale, I got more DNA matches every day.

As we were stuck in this rut, another new DNA match appeared on Ancestry.com—a third cousin with higher DNA numbers than anyone I currently matched. Could this be the clue we'd been waiting for? I sent this unknown DNA match an email and reached the daughter of my DNA match. She manages her mom's DNA kit, and she was eager to help in any way. Wow, what a relief this was, someone else willing to help. After months of going nowhere, maybe we would finally get closer, and we had someone who was willing to help.

I realized that on the website 23andMe, I matched DNA to the daughter who had agreed to help. Apparently, she did one DNA kit with 23andMe and her mother did another DNA kit with Ancestry.com. This now meant I match DNA to both of them. Since they are each on a different website, this gave us the opportunity to search their shared DNA matches on two websites. This could help, since each website has different people who have done DNA. We were hoping this would give us more leads. Who is the common ancestor to link all of this? More work began for Janet and me.

Janet and I finally managed to find a common ancestor and determine the two family surname lines I connect DNA with. Now to figure who from these lines could be my biological father.

This all came about because of the last few DNA matches. Now, just to figure out how and who is my biological father. Weeks went by and we added more to the working tree. By chance I decided to send an email to a woman named Susan who I saw had a tree on Ancestry.com. Susan also was listed in a few obituaries linked to these families we needed to research. We were not exactly sure who her parents were, and we needed to figure that out. Susan had her grandparents listed; they were two people from whom we still needed information about their children. I explained in the email why and what I was trying to solve. Never in a million years did I think this woman could help so much. The pieces of the puzzle and the two family surnames kept clicking together after our initial contact.

Susan had first sent me an email response fairly quickly. She asked if we could talk on the phone the next day. Of course, I said yes and eagerly awaited her call. What information did she have for me? How did she fall into the tree? Who were her parents?

The conversation was a bit surprising. Not only one, but both of her brothers had been in the military. My mother did tell me my biological father was in the military and other small details. Both of Susan's brothers were stationed at the same base where my mother worked. Could this be the answer? Susan filled me in on the details of her family. Her mom had married twice, and only now were the surnames all linking together. The tree was solving the puzzle. Susan explained to me that her kids had given her a DNA kit for Christmas and she had not mailed it to Ancestry.com until she received my initial email. Curiosity made her complete and mail her DNA sample. She also wondered if we were related.

We waited several weeks for Susan's DNA to return. The results showed up on Ancestry.com on a Saturday morning. Susan was indeed related to me; her DNA numbers on Ancestry.com showed her match as a first cousin. However, looking at the charts of chromosome numbers we determined she is actually my half-aunt. Wow! Did we just solve the case? I was a bit shocked, as Janet was also. This long search had finally paid off. One of her half-brothers must be my biological father. The only way one of her half-brothers could not be my biological father would be if one of their mother's sisters had an affair with their mother's husband. Quite a confusing scenario, but anything is still possible. I still keep that in my brain, anything is possible.

It had been a long process, long hours of hard, determined work and hundreds of emails to DNA matches. Had Janet and I finally solved the case? Both of us were very excited as the days passed.

Susan has two half-brothers. Which one could be my biological father? With her help it was determined it had to be Roger. Roger was still alive. He was stationed where my mother worked at the time I would have been conceived.

Funny thing, Janet and I had mapped so many of my DNA matches and expanded the working tree so much we already had Roger's father and stepmother listed in the tree. However, we did not have Roger's father's first wife listed, who is Susan's mother. We were that close a year ago and did not know. It took one email to Susan to fill in the blanks and solve the mystery. She linked the two surnames, and my DNA matches put the pieces together. Now, knowing all of this, where do I go?

Susan told me she wanted to tell Roger the news, but she informed me that they did not have a close relationship. Susan did not think he would take this news very well. After a year and a half of searching, I wanted this to go right. This has been my journey and life. I thought to myself over and over, should I be the one telling Roger? Do I write a letter? Susan wanted to tell him first. She

160

thought it would be better coming from her. It could help pave the path for me after the initial shock was over. But I kept thinking, if they were not close siblings, was this a good idea? I decided I would write Roger a letter.

Janet and I searched the Internet for any information we could find based on the information Susan had already provided. She had not given me Roger's address. I did not want to ask for it. Janet found Roger's address; it didn't take her long. The Internet is a great tool, but a bit scary in all the information you can piece together about someone. It only takes detective skills.

Susan emailed me and had made arrangements to meet Roger on Saturday, only a week away. On Saturday, I waited all day to hear from her. The waiting for this news was harder than waiting for DNA results. My wife and I stayed busy that day. After dinner, I still had not heard any news. Sunday, I still did not hear from Susan all afternoon. Did something happen? Why was she not calling to tell me? Did she not care that I had been waiting so long for this answer? Finally, later in the evening on Sunday, Susan called.

Just as she had suspected, he did not take the news well. He was not very nice to Susan, apparently. He did not deny anything but would not agree to a DNA test. I think the older generation is scared of all the new technology. I just want the truth here. Before Susan went to talk to Roger, I decided I would mail the letter I had written to him. I knew the letter would get to him a few days after they spoke.

I spent a few hours writing what I thought was the perfect letter to break the news that he is my biological father. I sent the letter by certified mail. Now the wait began again. Would he sign for the mail or not? Was he curious about who I am? Or was he really an ass?

About five days passed, and he did receive and sign for the letter. I had tracking on certified mail, so I could see when it was received. Knowing he got my letter does make me feel a little better, even if he is an ass. I did my part by telling him I exist. How he chooses to accept that is his journey.

I don't know what will happen in the future. I don't know if Roger will contact me or not. I do know that the man I call "Dad" is a good man and I would not change the results of my childhood. I had a good childhood and a good father. I will say, I hope my mother gets peace before she leaves this world. I will probably never understand how and why she did what she did, and all the secrets she kept. I do believe that she will come back in another life to learn some important lessons. I hope it will be the lesson of love and commitment to one person. We all deserve to have a happy life and have that one special person. I will always love the two parents that raised me, even through all this craziness.

The other surprise in this family is I have two half-brothers. I reached out to one, and we shall see what happens. I hope he will do a DNA test to prove what we already know.

My life is still like a *Seinfeld* episode. You never expect the ending. I still don't know what to expect.

THE END

P.S.: He sent in his DNA.

Chapter 33: Closure

Fifty-two years old and finding the man who raised me is not my biological father. In fact, I have discovered my three siblings and I all have different fathers. What a shocking journey this has been. Spending hours and hours on the computer searching all the DNA sites, just looking for clues and a DNA match to help tell me who my biological father is. I have solved all my siblings' mysteries. They all now know who their biological father is.

My mother's lack of help continued. Her health and dementia seemed to get worse with each passing day. That road to information was ending.

I ended Chapter 32 with "P.S. He sent in his DNA," referring to Susan's nephew Ryan. I was able to locate him with a little detective work. Let me explain. After getting the names of two possible half-brothers, I was able to track down through Facebook someone I thought was my half-brother Ryan. Ryan appeared on his mother's Facebook page with a woman I suspected was his girlfriend. I knew who Ryan's mother was because of all my research. I could not find Ryan anywhere on Facebook—maybe he didn't have an account? I started searching Facebook for Ryan's presumed girlfriend.

I decided to take a chance and contact this unknown woman through Facebook Messenger. Bingo! She was Ryan's girlfriend, and I did have the right family connection. Her name is Megan. Using Facebook Messenger, I asked her if she knew Ryan. She asked me if I was related to him. I told her it was a lot to explain on Messenger and asked if she would call me. Megan agreed and called my cell phone right away.

Feeling nervous as I answered the phone, I told her straightforward, "I believe Ryan is my half-brother." "Holy shit!"

was Megan's response. She was very kind and told me Ryan was working, and she would tell him everything when he got home. We had a long, pleasant conversation about the details of me searching for my biological father and my belief that Roger was Ryan's biological father and mine as well. Megan told me Ryan would probably need time to process all this new information and would probably call me back in a few days. I told her I understood the need to process the information. We said our goodbyes.

A few days had passed when Ryan called. He was nice, and not surprised that his father could have had other children out in the world. He informed me of family details I did not know. He told me I have another half-brother from Roger's first marriage, Roger Jr. Ryan's mother was Roger Sr.'s second wife. Ryan explained that, unfortunately, Roger Jr. was probably in jail somewhere because of a drug addiction problem. Ryan explained that he tries to distance himself from this half-brother because he did not need Roger Jr.'s problems coming into his life. Apparently, the family had tried many times to help Roger Jr. with his addiction by sending him to treatment programs, but Roger Jr. always seemed to fail at recovery. At this point in time, Ryan had no idea where Roger Jr. was living. We talked for a long time on the phone. It seemed weird that I was talking to my potential half-brother. I still didn't trust anything until DNA tests showed the results. Talking to Ryan was something I never expected to happen in my lifetime. It was hard to believe that, at fifty-two years old, I could have two more half-siblings. I wasn't sure I would ever find the answer to "Who is my biological father?"

I had sent Roger, my potential biological father, a certified letter. I knew he received the letter because I had a tracking number, and he signed for the letter. Why was Roger not contacting me? I wished I knew that answer. I told Ryan about the certified letter and lack of response. Ryan could not explain his father's behavior and told me his father had never said a word about me or the letter.

When our conversation ended, we left it that we would chat again soon. After the conversation, I talked with my wife, Laurie. She has been here for me through this entire process. I wanted to tell her about Ryan and the new discoveries he told me. I was excited to have a potential younger brother and the possibility of getting to know him. I couldn't sleep. I tossed and turned, as my head was spinning. Was this the end of the long journey? Or just a new beginning?

Ryan and I continued to talk and text. I could tell we are similar in many ways. We both use humor. Both of us are smart-asses. We exchanged many jokes about our new discovery of each other. Ryan agreed to do an Ancestry DNA kit. He wanted to know if we were half-siblings; after all, I did match DNA to his Aunt Susan.

Megan, Ryan's girlfriend, called to tell me Ryan was in the hospital with kidney stones. I asked her if Ryan still agreed to do the DNA test. I told Megan I would pay for a kit and get it mailed to him right away. Probably not the right time to ask for DNA, when Ryan is in excruciating pain. Still, I did ask. I knew he would find humor in that despite his circumstances. He agreed to do the test. While in the hospital he laughed and made a comment that I'd better be his half-sister, because I am a pain in the ass. I just laughed.

I ordered a DNA kit from Ancestry and it shipped to his home address. Now the wait began again. I had waited for so long; you would think I would be used to it by now. It was still not an easy thing to do.

Ryan's DNA results were in after several weeks. It was confirmed: He is my half-brother. All the searching Janet and I did finally paid off. I have confirmed DNA and another half-sibling—

well, really two, if Roger Jr. is really Roger Sr.'s biological son. I felt nervous knowing for a DNA fact that Roger is my biological father. He is my father and Ryan's father. Wow! What a ride this has been. Emotions up and down, the stress of not knowing until now.

Now what? What do we do with all of this? I guessed the next conversation I had with Ryan would lead us in the direction life was supposed to take us. I was so happy and nervous all at the same time. Now I needed to meet my half-brother. Did we look alike? What were his interests? We knew we both had the same smart-ass humor. So many thoughts in my brain again. We exchanged several pictures by text. We did look alike. It was crazy to see our baby pictures and other later ones next to each other. Sharing pictures of us as we aged was eye-opening. We looked so much alike. Me, the female version of him and he, the male version of me. I do have short hair!

Laurie and I made plans to meet Ryan for the first time. We got our plane tickets and found a really cool hotel overlooking a minor league baseball stadium in Manchester, New Hampshire. Too bad it was not baseball season. It would have been fun to watch a game. A few weeks passed and our meeting date was getting closer. Ryan and I had been chatting on the phone and texting often. It felt really cool to have a younger brother; I was excited to meet him. Maybe this sibling relationship would be a closer one. Maybe he needed an older sister. Our Aunt Susan and her husband were also going to meet us at the hotel.

What could go wrong? A storm, a damn hurricane coming up the east coast! Laurie and I had to cancel our trip. Was this a sign of things to come? Flights all over were being canceled, and now we would have to reschedule this trip. Another *Seinfeld* episode in the story of my life. Always something crazy to stop me in my tracks. We would have to wait a few months to reschedule because of prior engagements. This was not at all what I wanted, again more waiting! No one can ever say I don't have patience. My patience in this life has been tested over and over. If there is such a thing as reincarnation, I will not need to learn the lesson of patience. Cross that off my lesson plan. Been there, done that!

Ryan and I continued to talk on the phone and get to know each other. I still had not told my other siblings that I had solved my own mystery and now knew who my biological father is. I'm not sure why I was waiting— I think because I didn't want to jinx anything. Then there is the fact that I am not really close with my siblings. I wished my friend Karen was living and I could talk to her. She was probably on the other side smiling that I found the answer. I do believe she is with me. This had been a long journey for me, and I wanted everything to go well. This journey is about me, not my other siblings, I told myself. I sometimes didn't know how to feel with all this new information, information I had searched for without giving up. Sometimes my brain felt like it was on overload. I guess, like the old saying goes, don't ask unless you want to know. I was in the no-turning-back stage now. I now knew the truth; Roger is my biological father. I felt torn because Roger was not contacting me. I asked myself so many questions. Was he hoping I would go away after my letter? It was all so confusing with him. Had his rejection of me started without him knowing me? I still was shocked that my dad, the man who raised me, was not my biological father. Who the hell would think I would be a retired cop solving my own family's secrets in my fifties? Are there more family secrets to be found?

Ryan and Aunt Susan had both sent me pictures of Roger, old pictures and newer ones. It was strange for me to now see pictures of a man I resemble. I always wanted to see a picture of my biological father, since starting this crazy journey. Now, I couldn't believe it was happening. He and I do have a lot of similar features. Now, I

167

really understood how my adoptive friends felt when they saw a picture of their biological parent for the first time. I knew I looked like my mom, but now I saw my biological father's photos, and we had many similarities. We have a face dimple in the same location, and I have his eyes and cheeks. It was now so real, seeing pictures.

Laurie and I sat back and laughed at all of this. We found the humor in my mom's affairs and all my siblings having different fathers. All the discoveries in the last two years. I really don't know how I have done this. Maybe humor makes it okay? You can't change things. Humor was the one thing Ryan and I definitely had in common, in our own way. I wondered if the humor was meant to cover up the sadness of the family. My mind was constantly running on all these thoughts. I thought a comedy series of my life would make a great new show on Netflix.

Ryan and I were raised in completely different ways. I feel he lacked the bonding of a father, which I had; both our mothers were very caring. I only wish he had a fun-filled childhood like I did. It seems he grew up very quickly and had early-life responsibilities and worries. That is not the way a child is supposed to grow up. I saw a saying that goes like this: A child's shoulders were not built to bear the weight of their parents' choices. I always liked this. I feel this fits Ryan more than me. I was able to be a child without responsibility and worry. I thank my parents for that.

I did not tell my mother I found my biological father. I showed her a picture of him in his younger days and asked if she recognized him. She only commented that he was a good-looking man. I tried not to laugh. I really wanted to say, he'd better be good-looking, you slept with him and as a result here I am. I just kept my comments to myself, which was hard to do. But because of my mom's health, I still wanted to protect her and her feelings. I thought to myself, what good would it do? Would she even understand?

Maybe it would make me feel better? I didn't know the answer. Just something else to think about.

We planned a new trip to New Hampshire. A few days before our trip Ryan and I were talking on the phone. I told him I thought he should tell Roger, our father, I was coming to town. I wanted to give Roger an opportunity to meet me. I wanted to see if he would. He still hadn't responded to the certified letter. My curiosity to know him was getting stronger. I told Ryan that I wished he would tell Roger that he knew about me, and we were in contact. Maybe coming from Ryan, Roger would feel more at ease with the subject. Ryan said he had thought about it, but Roger was in a bad mood the last time he talked to him. I explained to Ryan that I hoped he would tell Roger he and I were going to have a sister-brother relationship. I could tell Ryan felt like this was necessary, but I suspected the thought of the conversation with Roger was awkward for him. It seemed the family was lacking in the communication process. We ended our phone conversation and acknowledged that we would see each other in a few days. About an hour's time had passed when Ryan called back and said, "I have an early Christmas present for you." He told me Roger was coming to lunch with us on Saturday. Wow, I couldn't believe it! Ryan told me I owe him a lot of past years of missed Christmas gifts. We both laughed. I was just shocked that he even called Roger and told him I was coming to town. I hadn't seen that coming.

On a Friday in November 2018 Laurie and I flew to New Hampshire to meet my half-brother Ryan, half-aunt Susan, and my biological father. No hurricane in the forecast this time. I felt nervous and excited, and hoped everything would go well. Our plane was on time as we arrived in Manchester, New Hampshire. We got a rental car and headed toward the hotel. Ryan, his girlfriend, Megan, Aunt Susan, and Susan's husband were meeting us at the hotel at

7:00 p.m. We were to have dinner at the hotel restaurant. It was raining really hard as we got the rental car. A normally fifteen-minute drive took us over an hour; it didn't help that we missed our exit and went way out of our way. Another adventure for Laurie and me. We just laughed. We got lost and were going to be late. All I could think was, of course this is happening. It's my crazy world.

We finally made it to the hotel safely. As we walked in, Susan spotted us and came over and gave me a huge hug. She said, "I can't believe this is happening and is real." Laurie said hello and headed to check us into our room. We quickly took our luggage to the room and went back downstairs to meet with Aunt Susan and her husband. We got a table in the restaurant, which was right off the hotel lobby. Ryan was running late. We sat down and started chatting. It felt like I had known Aunt Susan a long time. I felt very comfortable. Having some wine, I felt even more relaxed. I had two heavy pours.

Ryan and Megan showed up. We all hugged and sat down at the table. I couldn't believe how much he and I resembled one another. Pictures are one thing, but in person we really did look alike. We all chatted for hours and hours. We even told the waitress we were meeting for the first time. She was shocked and excited for our story. Ryan and I gave her a quick, Reader's Digest version of how we found out we were siblings. It was a great night, chatting and getting to know each other. After midnight we said our goodbyes, and Ryan and Megan left to drive about an hour home in the rain. We would see each other for lunch the next day, in nearby Massachusetts. Aunt Susan and her husband were staying the night at the hotel, so they didn't have to drive home in the rain after dark. I totally understood that, I can't see to drive at night these days either, especially in rain. Laurie always drives us at night and laughs that I can't see, and I am younger than she.

So excited we all met, I couldn't get much sleep. My heart was full of gratitude. I couldn't stop thinking that Ryan made arrangements for Roger to meet us for lunch the next day. I was going to meet my biological father for the first time. I was fifty-two years old now, and this still was very shocking to me. To think the man that raised me was not my biological father. I was in New Hampshire! Questions to ask this stranger ran through my head all night. How would he react? Did he date my mother? How did they meet? Did he know about me? Was it a one-night thing? So many thoughts, so many answers I wanted. My brain was going in all different directions. Usually, I am the one who puts my head on the pillow and is asleep within ten seconds. Laurie always tells me she has never known someone who falls asleep so fast. Well, that was not happening. It was a toss-and-turn night for me.

Morning arrived and we met Aunt Susan and her husband downstairs for breakfast at the hotel. Aunt Susan was still shocked that she had a niece. I think the entire thing was a bit overwhelming for both of us. We had another pleasant conversation over breakfast. I was a bit nervous this morning because I knew in a few hours I would meet Roger for the first time.

Around eleven in the morning Laurie and I headed to Massachusetts in our rental car. We found the restaurant where we were going to meet. My belly was still so full from breakfast, and being nervous, I didn't know how I could eat. Laurie and I went inside and got a table. Laurie asked me what I would say. I really had no idea, other than "Surprise!" You'd think I would have had an entire speech ready in my head. I told Laurie I had to pee, and she said, "Don't you leave me here alone. I don't want him to think I am you." We both laughed. About ten minutes had gone by when I saw Ryan and who I believed was Roger walking behind him. Ryan waved, and they came toward us. I did the first thing that came into my brain: I stood up and said, "Surprise!" Roger looked at me and gave me a big hug. I could tell by his eyes that he was touched but at a loss for words. After all, I had had almost two years to process this information. He had had only about four months. But then again, I didn't want to make excuses for him; he had had every opportunity to contact me after he read my certified letter. He never attempted to contact me. I did hold a bit of anger.

We all exchanged pleasantries. I gave him my book, *Exposed by DNA*. Originally it was finished in 2018. This "Closure" chapter was written in 2021 to bring the story to an end. I told Roger, "This is my story searching for you." Inside the book I had written a personal note for Roger. He and Ryan both read what I had written and got tears in their eyes. I guess I was a bit shocked and, of course, what came blurting out of my mouth but "Are you both crying?" I then laughed, but it was a nervous laugh, I didn't know how to react. I shared pictures with Roger of me as an infant and one of me in my police uniform. He asked if he could keep the pictures. I was happy he wanted them and said yes. I knew Roger liked to play golf, so I gave him some Maryland logo golf balls. Of course, since we had eaten a huge breakfast, Laurie and I were not very hungry. We ended up getting one dish and splitting it. We all sat and chatted for about two hours before leaving the restaurant. Laurie and I followed Ryan and Roger back to Ryan's house so we could all sit down and talk more.

Ryan had a cute house, and I loved the fact that he lived directly across from a huge cemetery. He had a cute rescue pit bull who was super sweet, and of course I love dogs. We took a few group pictures of all of us and then a few pictures of Roger and me, and me with Ryan. When viewing the pictures, we could see that we all have very similar features. This was just so real now.

A few hours passed as we talked. I shared with Roger a lot of the family history I discovered while searching to find him. He shared a few stories about his parents and siblings. He still seemed very cautious in what he shared, leaving me with a somewhat distant feeling. I found that interesting. I seemed to know more about the genealogy of his family than he did. Ryan did not know much history on his father's side other than basic information he had been told. I shared a lot of the information I had discovered with both of them. It was getting close to dinner time, and Laurie and I still had to drive the unknown roads back to the hotel in New Hampshire. We said our goodbyes and planned to stay in touch. It was weird to me saying goodbye. I guess I had somewhat of a scenario planned for my reunion with Roger and Ryan. It was not what I had imagined. Ryan was more caring and accepting. I wasn't sure what Roger thought. Was he freaked out that he had a gay daughter? I have been out of the "closet" since my teen years, and am very happy and married. Was this an issue for him? Could he have known about me all along? Did he know my mom was pregnant way back then, and he was my father? He didn't ask many questions about my life, which seemed odd to me. The only thing he did say, in a funny comment, was what the title of my next book should be. He and my mother apparently used to have lunch dates on Fridays. He thought I should call it *Lunch Date*.

In the morning I chatted with Ryan a bit on the phone. Laurie and I had plans to do a bit of sightseeing. We wanted to see Salem, Massachusetts, and the witch stuff there. We sat in on a mock witch trial, which was narrated and done very well. Afterward, we walked around the town and had lunch. Our waitress was very nice, and we even shared with her a little bit about why we were in Massachusetts, and me finding my half-brother. She told me she would buy my book. As we started to head back to the hotel in New

Hampshire, I contacted Ryan to see what he was doing the rest of the day. We were about twenty minutes from his house, and I wanted to see him again. He invited us to come back to his house and hang out. Laurie and I did exactly that. It would be good to spend more time getting to know him. While we were at his house, Ryan told me the one big difference between us: He was a Republican and I was a Democrat. He made it clear that he was all red, no matter what. I was a little surprised he was bringing up politics. I guess he remembered in my book I mentioned my political views. I started to realize our morals and values did not match at all. He said some things I was shocked about. I didn't care for our current Republican president; Ryan thought he was great. I wasn't sure how that would affect our sibling bond. I have voted for a Republican, just not "that guy." I didn't know how anyone could have any respect for a bully. He was not a leader, just a reality TV star, not a president.

At this point I didn't say too much about it. I really wanted to see where this relationship was headed. I had fought too hard for women's rights, gay marriage, and equal rights. I was not going backward. I didn't know Ryan very well, and he did not know me. We both had our strong beliefs. I will never lose my own values for anyone, and I do fight for what I believe. This relationship or lack of a relationship would be interesting. We said our goodbyes and left.

Laurie and I made it back home safe and sound. All quiet on the home front. Apparently, my mother and father had made out okay while we were gone. No emergencies had happened. They probably didn't remember we were gone. My father thought we went north to see friends. My mother probably didn't remember we were gone. Every day could be different, with her dementia.

We have learned to hate our home phone ringing at night. Between my parents' emergency night calls and Laurie's uncle calling, we have had our fill. Nothing like the phone scaring the shit out of you at two in the morning. Laurie's Uncle Bob would call our home phone in the middle of the night, scaring the crap out of us. When Laurie answered, Uncle Bob would act like it was daytime and just start chatting. We would both be shocked, and our hearts would be racing for hours after the call. No sleep on those nights. However, Uncle Bob was the kindest soul. It would make us laugh the next day, but in the middle of the night, that ring would make our hearts jolt. Caller ID can be the worst thing sometimes, seeing the number in the middle of the night. Your first thoughts: What's wrong? What has happened?

I guess I kind of understand now what parents go through with their kids out all night— the worry of the phone call. They say we become our parents as we get older, and getting even older we become the child. I think they are both right. I worry that my parents are the children now. I don't have kids, and this is not what I ever imagined as I got older.

On a visit with my mother, I told her I had met Roger. She looked confused, but it was hard to say what she was thinking because she still held that secret in her soul. She acted curious as I told her about our trip. She didn't ask any questions, just listened to me talk. I just didn't get it; I was a grown adult, and I had told her that I found him. What was there still to hide? I still ponder that. I wished that she would just tell me about him. Never any luck with that wish.

Thanksgiving and then Christmas passed. Both Ryan and Roger called at each holiday to say hello. This was all so new to me. My own siblings in Maryland don't even call me on a holiday. Family is so damn weird and unpredictable. Laurie and a few other family members met for lunch at the facility where my mom now lived. The staff had a nice meal for all the residents and their families. My mother was in an okay mood at first, but then was

175

ready to go back to her room. She was ready for all of us to leave. I didn't know if this was all overwhelming to her. But then again, as my mom got older, she really didn't like to socialize, even with her own family. She missed many family gatherings and would make excuses not to go. Guilt, perhaps? She didn't really call her friends either, and she became more of a recluse. I know she thought her life was over because of the Parkinson's diagnosis. She changed quickly.

Laurie and I decided that since it was still early on Christmas Day, we should go try our luck at the casino. We love the casino. It paid off—I won five thousand dollars on a quarter slot machine. Merry Christmas to us. We laughed in excitement. We are very lucky together, and that day proved it once again. I was surprised at how many people were at the casino on Christmas Day. We never thought it would be crowded.

Funny, I found out my biological father also likes to go to casinos. When we got home, I texted Ryan to tell him I won. Ryan told me he never was that lucky. Of course, I responded, "With a bad attitude, you won't ever win."

I'm going to skip ahead in time. It has been over a year since I talked to Roger, my biological father. He never calls to say hello or check in on me anymore. I have left messages for him. He called in February 2020 to say he was sorry to hear that my mom had passed away. My mom passed away in December 2019. I guess the call was better late than never. Ryan must have told Roger at some point about my mom, since they do talk. I don't really know when he found out about my mom's death. He never asked anything about my mom's health or anything, even after I talked about her. Friends I have not talked to in years called and sent sympathy cards to me after my mom died. I believe Roger lacks in compassion. Maybe because his parents were awful to him, or so I've heard. Family traits seem to pass onto next generations. My conversations with Roger, when we did have them, were very superficial. How's the weather? Have you been to the casino? He never asked about my wife or family or anything personal.

I talked to my parents many times in a week, if only to check in and see if they needed anything. It's so weird for me to understand the communication—or should I say lack of communication—between Roger and Ryan, and now me. I don't get it, and probably never will. They do not have a close relationship. I can't imagine having a kid and not wanting to be involved in their life. Roger doesn't talk to his own siblings. My Aunt Susan, who helped me find Roger in the beginning, has not spoken to him since the day she told him about me in 2018. Roger's brother, my newfound uncle, calls me and always tells me he wishes I was his child not Roger's. He is nothing like his brother, my biological father.

Ryan told me that Roger's not calling me has to do with his third wife. She thinks I want something from them. I got the impression Roger and his third wife are both selfish and think everyone always wants something. Maybe because they always want something from people, their own selfishness comes out? I want nothing from them. I have never met his third wife. Roger never even talked about his wife to me. Both Ryan and I have made our own success in life and need nothing. I actually feel sorry for Roger.

I stay in touch with Ryan here and there. Roger completely disappeared. Apparently, he moved to Florida, according to Ryan. Aunt Susan and I text now and then. I wish it was a fairy-tale ending. But at least I found the answers and never gave up. I will always say this to anyone searching: Never give up.

My parents are my parents, and I will always treasure both of them. Roger is just an affair my mom had, a sperm donor. I guess the lesson I have learned is, life does throw you curve balls. I am so happy my life took this path and I had two great parents.

Made in the USA
Middletown, DE
06 May 2024

53927841R00106